The Healthy Church is a must for any active or would-be pastor. The diagnosis of the nine diseases that infect today's churches can save us all a lot of heartache if we will take heed to these warnings. I will want to keep this book on my desk and use it to check the pulse of our church on a consistent basis. Thank you, Peter Wagner!

TED HAGGARD
Pastor, New Life Church, Colorado Springs

The Healthy Church is the kind of diagnostic guide all Christian leaders should have on hand in their ecclesiastical medicine chest.

THE REV. RICHARD KEW AND
RT. REV. ROGER WHITE
Russian Ministry Network

Peter Wagner has written an extraordinary book about preventing nine painful diseases that can afflict your church. His unique insight will help your church build up a "healthy immune system" and offers treatments for these destructive diseases. *The Healthy Church* will breathe life into any church.

DR. JOHN MAXWELL
Founder, INJOY, Inc.

The passage of time brings illnesses to both people and churches. *The Healthy Church* supplies the criteria for making both a diagnosis and a customized prescription. This may be Peter Wagner's best book!

LYLE E. SCHALLER
Author, Parish Consultant

This book is great—Peter Wagner at his best. He has applied the problems of growth to today's cultures, examining the consequences of not applying spiritual factors to growth. *The Healthy Church* is for the whole Body of Christ.

ELMER L. TOWNS
Dean of the School of Religion, Liberty University

THE
HEALTHY
CHURCH

C. PETER WAGNER

Regal

A Division of Gospel Light
Ventura, California, U.S.A.

Published by Regal Books
A Division of Gospel Light
Ventura, California, U.S.A.
Printed in U.S.A.

Regal Books is a ministry of Gospel Light, an evangelical Christian publisher
dedicated to serving the local church. We believe God's vision for Gospel Light
is to provide church leaders with biblical, user-friendly materials that will help
them evangelize, disciple and minister to children, youth and families.

It is our prayer that this Regal book will help you discover biblical truth for your
own life and help you meet the needs of others. May God richly bless you.

For a free catalog of resources from Regal Books/Gospel Light please contact your
Christian supplier or call 1-800-4-GOSPEL.

Library of Congress Cataloging-in-Publication Data
Wagner, C. Peter.
    The healthy church / C. Peter Wagner.
        p. cm.
    Includes bibliographical references and index.
    ISBN 0-8307-1861-3 (trade paper)
    1. Church growth. 2. Church renewal. I. Title.
BV652.25.W323 1996   96-8946
250—dc20   CIP

1 2 3 4 5 6 7 8 9 10 11 12 13 14 15 16 17 / 03 02 01 00 99 98 97 96

Rights for publishing this book in other languages are contracted by Gospel
Literature International (GLINT). GLINT also provides technical help for the adap-
tation, translation and publishing of Bible study resources and books in scores of
languages worldwide. For further information, contact GLINT, P.O. Box 4060,
Ontario, CA 91761-1003, U.S.A., or the publisher.

Contents

INTRODUCTION

It would be nice if churches were never sick. Many, I am glad to report, are not. This is not to say that any would be considered either by themselves or by outside observers as being *perfect*. It is not uncommon, however, to find churches that are fairly normal, that are growing and that function from day to day more or less the way God designed them. Others, unfortunately, are not what they really should be, except perhaps in the most minimal way. It is not inaccurate to describe such churches as sick.

As I write this book, I am completing three decades of studying the life, health and growth of churches. I love the Church, reflecting, I hope, the love of Jesus Christ for what the Bible describes as His bride. I rejoice about healthy churches, and I grieve about sick churches. My desire is that sick churches will recover their health and join the others in being all that God expects them to be. That is why I am writing this book.

As you read, you will find descriptions of nine church diseases. Some of the names may be unfamiliar to you, but the names are not intended to be gimmicks or attention-grabbing sermon points. These nine diseases occur and reoccur with disturbing frequency. During the years that I have been testing these concepts with church leaders of virtually every denomination, I have found widespread agreement that these maladies are easily recognized, and that their symptoms generally fall into patterns that do not vary much from church to church.

I am not attempting to develop a complete pathology of church diseases. Certainly, many more diseases exist than the nine I have chosen. These nine, however, are identifiable specifically as *growth-inhibiting diseases*. My professional role is as a professor of church growth, and therefore I use much of my energy in attempting to discover what helps churches grow and what hinders churches from growing. The nine diseases in this book fall into the latter category.

My first book about church diseases was published nearly 20 years ago. Since then much has changed, but the essential character of the diseases has not, any more than the character of human diseases changes from generation to generation. I wish I could report that we had since discovered a spiritual equivalent to the Salk vaccine, which has virtually eliminated polio, but I cannot. A major change did come in my own life and ministry during those years, however, and my former list of eight diseases has now become nine—the addition is "hypopneumia," an abnormally low level of spiritual power. I previously was looking at churches through the lenses of a weak theology of the Holy Spirit.

If your church has been experiencing growth problems, it is my prayer that God will use this book to help you understand them, overcome them and see the new life and vigor you desire pour into your church and bless your community.

Chapter 1

Can Christ's Body Be Sick?

The Bible calls the Church the "body of Christ." The apostle Paul said that God puts all things under Jesus' feet and makes Him the head of "the church, which is His body" (Eph. 1:22,23).

Now I fully realize that biblical analogies must not be pushed too far. Through my decades of research about the growth and nongrowth of churches here in America and around the world, however, I clearly discovered, much to my dismay, that some churches in their present condition apparently *cannot* grow. I kept asking the question: Why?

HEALTH AND GROWTH

It seems that one of the signs of good church health is growth. If a given church is faithful to the Lord, and if it is in a healthy condition, God can be expected to do what He did to the Church that came into being on the Day of Pentecost. He will ordinarily add "to the church daily those who [are] being saved" (Acts 2:47). Seeing new people come to Christ and commit themselves to the Body of Christ is normal for healthy Christian churches.

As we all know, however, some churches that are faithful to God do not seem to grow. They confess Jesus as Lord. They believe in sound doctrine. They pray with fervor. They study the Bible and conscientiously seek to obey its precepts. They raise funds for foreign missions. They serve their fellow human beings. They celebrate the Lord's Supper regularly. Somehow, though, their faithfulness to God, of and by itself, does not seem to be attractive enough to outsiders to draw them into the church. With a few exceptions, the church consists of virtually the same group of people as it was 5 or 10 years ago.

By pointing this out, I am not drawing the lines between the "true church" and some kind of false church. I have been misunderstood by some to contend that growth in membership is one of the signs of the true church. I can see how this might have happened, because I am extremely enthusiastic about promoting church growth, but I hope that I would never allow myself to fall into such theological naiveté. God loves faithful churches whether or not they grow. To put it another way, Jesus loves His bride.

MAKING IT HARD TO GO TO HELL

At the same time, I want to make it clear that, in certain exceptions such as churches suffering from ghost town disease (see chapter 3), churches that are not seeing unbelievers come to Christ through their ministries regularly are missing out on something God desires for them. The members of that church might be doctrinally sound and on their way to heaven, but what influence are they having on their community? I like the subtitle of Pastor Ted Haggard's book *Primary Purpose*. It says: *Making It Hard for People to Go to Hell from Your City.*

Ted Haggard, pastor of the New Life Church of Colorado Springs, takes this so seriously that he has his church receptionist cut the obituaries from the local newspaper each morning and photocopy them for each church staff member. Attached to each one is a Post-it Note that reads: "Today from Colorado Springs people will go to heaven, and people will go to hell. The percentage of people going to heaven and the percentage of people going to hell today is determined by how well you did your job yesterday."[1] This language might be blunter than some pastors would choose to use, but Haggard is telling it like it is!

SOME GROW AND SOME DON'T

As if on some kind of cue, most of the major denominations in the United States began losing members in 1965. Almost all had grown, some vigorously, during the previous 20 years. The United Methodist Church, the Presbyterian Church (U.S.A.), the Episcopal Church, the Disciples of Christ, the United Church of Christ, the Evangelical Lutheran Church of America, the Reformed Church of America and many others were once called America's "mainline" denominations. After 30 years of steady decline, they are now frequently referred to as the "old line" denominations.

Not every denomination in the United States, though, has lost membership during the past 30 years. Good growth has occurred in the Assemblies of God, the Southern Baptists, the Church of the Nazarene, the Christian and Missionary Alliance, the Evangelical Free Church of America, the Church of God (Cleveland, Tenn.) and many others, most notably among what are now called "new apostolic" churches.

In virtually every sizable metropolitan area of the country, a predictable phenomenon can occur. During the same time period and in the same place, some churches grow, others decline and die and still others stay about the same year after year. The question in the minds of those who carefully observe this state of affairs is: What are the differences between the growing as opposed to the nongrowing churches?

CHURCH GROWTH IS COMPLEX

Church growth is always complex. By this I do not mean that understanding the true causes of church growth and decline are beyond our grasp, but I do mean that the matter should not be oversimplified. Much too frequently, someone discovers what would sound, to all intents and purposes, as if it is a cure-all for church membership loss. "Is your church static? Just begin doing so-and-so and your church will turn around and grow. How do I know? My church was static, I did so-and-so, and it has been growing ever since." Unfortunately, there is

more to it than that. What is good for one church might not be
good for another one, even in the same denomination.

When the leaders of the old-line denominations began to realize that their membership losses were alarming, they convened
a high-level consortium to study the matter.[2] One of their conclusions, after two years of work, was that churches grow and
decline as a result of the interplay of four basic sets of factors.

1. *National contextual factors.* These relate to national trends
in population, attitudes, values and social conditions.

2. *National institutional factors.* These relate to policies determined on the denominational level concerning priorities of
ministry, theological stance, church polity and other areas that
to one degree or another affect all the churches in the denomination. On a smaller than national scale, these could also be
seen as *regional institutional factors,* influenced by decisions of
regional judicatories such as diocese, conferences, presbyter-
ies, synods, districts or the like.

3. *Local contextual factors.* This relates to social trends in the
local community, neighborhood or area where the church is
located.

4. *Local institutional factors.* These are conditions that exist
within the leadership and membership of the local church.

Some years after the conclusion of the work of the consortium, of which I happened to be a member, I felt compelled to
add a fifth set of factors to the list:

5. *Spiritual factors.* Because the growth or nongrowth of the
true church rests ultimately in the hands of God, the interrela-
tionship between what we do and what God does is of
supreme importance.

The focus of this book will be primarily about *local* institutional factors, *local* contextual factors, and *spiritual* factors. The
other sets of factors also have some bearing on church pathology, but my purpose in this book is to analyze growth and
nongrowth from the viewpoint of the health of the *local congregation,* not so much the national denomination or the
regional judicatory.

THE "BODY OF CHRIST"

This brings us back to the "body of Christ." As far as we know
from the Bible, Jesus Christ was never sick while He was on

earth. Theological reasoning supposes, however, that He could have been sick at some time or other. Christians believe that Jesus was fully human, while also being fully divine. Of course, He never did sin, and some might argue that this could have kept Him from ever being sick. We do not know that for sure. I must say, though, that if Jesus never had a headache or a cold or diarrhea he must have come a bit short of understanding what it was like to be human.

It is only natural to suppose that churches can be either sick or healthy, and that their health will influence their growth.

In any case, the Body of Christ today—the Church—is not free from sin. Nor is it free from sickness. I believe we do not stretch the biblical analogy too far to suppose that the Body of Christ can be sick, or it can be healthy. One of the indications of this is that although the membership of the United Methodist denomination, for example, was declining severely, many local United Methodist churches were growing vigorously. Obviously, some of their churches are healthy and some are sick. The same could be said about all other denominations.

My major concern is to discover and describe the reasons for this variance.

THE MEDICAL MODEL

As I mentioned at the beginning of this chapter, the Bible refers to the Church as the "body of Christ" (see Eph. 1:22,23). As this analogy is manifested in the Scriptures, we see that the Body of Christ has specific parts such as a head (see 4:15); joints (see v. 16); feet, hands, ears and eyes (see 1 Cor. 12:15-17); and "many members" (see Rom. 12:4). This Body, we are told, should be "built up" or "edified" (see Eph. 4:12). In other words, the Church should grow the way a body grows. If this is the case, it is only natural to suppose that churches can be either sick or healthy, and that their health will influence their growth.

The notion of relating church *growth* to church *health* has proved to be helpful to many church leaders. It is not entirely new. Many others have spoken of healthy or sick churches as being characterized by certain traits. Some have coined diseaselike names to prove a point they were making. For example, churches that think they need new buildings to sustain their growth have been stigmatized at times as having an "edifice complex." Hollis L. Green wrote a whole book about it, entitled *Why Churches Die* (Bethany Fellowship). The book contains 35 chapters, each describing a possible cause of weakness in a given local church.

SYSTEMATIZING
CHURCH PATHOLOGY

Few systematic and sustained efforts that I am aware of have attempted to develop what I would choose to call the field of "church pathology." Not much energy has been devoted to identifying, naming and analyzing crippling church diseases. Just thinking of an appropriate name for a disease can, in itself, begin a curing process called the "Rumpelstiltskin effect."

Through the years, I have found this to be true with many of the diseases listed in this book. Lights frequently are turned on when a church leader first hears the term "koinonitis" or "ethnikitis." Just the assurance that others in the past and in the present have experienced the same malady can remove much of the mystery, and consequently bring a therapeutic influence.

The pathology of church growth, curiously enough, has not been included in most seminary and Bible school curricula in the past. Possibly not a single minister in America has taken a full course in the subject. As a result, pastors in general tend to know little about the field, and their churches may be sick without their realizing it. Pastors also may suspect that their churches are sick, but are not able either to diagnose the disease or to prescribe a cure.

One of the encouraging signs is the recent emergence of a cadre of professional church diagnosticians whom I would like to call "ecclesiologists." A combination of aptitude, training and intuition has given these people an unusual ability to examine a church and accurately diagnose its health in as little as one day's time, given some previous research and measurements by the pastor.

Some of these ecclesiologists work in denominational offices and some are interdenominational. My hope is that eventually they will be as readily available to needy churches as physicians are to people in general. If this happens, massive declines in church membership such as we have been witnessing in our nation could be managed and arrested.

As the field of church health develops, pastors themselves will gain a sensitivity to the conditions of their own churches and will be able to diagnose many of the diseases themselves. The younger ones will be studying this in seminary and Bible school, as new textbooks for such a study are developed. The older ones will pick up professional training in the doctor of ministry and continuing education programs that are now proliferating in America.[3]

THF POSITIVE SIDE: VITAL SIGNS

When a body is functioning in a healthy way, its vital signs are in good shape. This is the positive side of health. Churches, like human beings, have vital signs that seem to be common among those that are healthy and growing. If the vital signs are known, efforts can be made to maintain them and avoid illness. This is the *preventive* medicine aspect of church health. Healthy churches build an immune system to resist disease. It is much more advisable to *prevent* an illness than to contract one and then have to *cure* it.

Although undoubtedly much more needs to be done in the field, I have made an attempt to analyze seven of the vital signs of healthy churches in my book *Your Church Can Grow* (Regal Books). That book, which has sold more than 150,000 copies, is an essential companion volume to this one. The following is a brief review of the vital signs, the positive side of church growth, before we go on with the negative side, that of pathology:

A Positive Pastor

The first vital sign of a healthy church is a pastor who is a possibility thinker and whose dynamic leadership has been used to catalyze the entire church into action for growth. Because I will have a good deal more to say about the pastor later on in this chapter, I will not elaborate further at this point.

A Well-Mobilized Laity

The second vital sign is a well-mobilized laity that has discovered, has developed and is using all the spiritual gifts for growth. Although laity can be mobilized in many ways, I believe nothing can improve on what are described in the Bible as spiritual gifts. Christians are to function as members of Christ's Body, and each person has been given a spiritual gift or gifts to do a certain job. Therefore, one of the most important spiritual exercises for a Christian is to discover, develop and use his or her spiritual gift.

Not only does knowing one's spiritual gift or gifts benefit each individual Christian, but it also provides the basic human resources necessary for a church to grow. Because church growth is complex, mobilizing spiritual gifts is not by itself sufficient to make any church grow, but it certainly is a factor of first-line priority.

Just how the mobilization of 27 spiritual gifts relates to growth dynamics in churches is developed in my book *Your Spiritual Gifts Can Help Your Church Grow* (Regal Books). Gospel Light publishes a reproducible group study guide that can be used, along with the book, in any church or home group for helping people discover their spiritual gifts. These valuable resources are available in your local Christian bookstore.

Meeting Members' Needs

The third vital sign of a healthy church is a church big enough to provide the range of services that meet the needs and expectations of its members. To be attractive to newcomers, a church has to serve its members well. If it does, it will produce satisfied customers, so to speak, who will in turn spread the news that the church is doing things that appeal to outsiders as well.

Some things can be done in churches of any size, such as bringing people to Christ, providing fellowship and pastoral care or offering Sunday School training for young children.

Other kinds of services require a larger "critical mass" to generate appeal. A strong ministry to single adults, for example, requires substantial numbers to be attractive. One of the slogans used by experts in this field is "singles go where singles are." A church of 200 or 300 probably won't have a dynamic singles ministry, so if ministering to singles is a community need the church wants to meet, the church must be fairly large to do an adequate job.

Some churches find small, relatively quiet worship services appealing. A congregation of 150 having few or no strangers

---

It is recommended that a church carefully examine the needs of the unchurched people around it, establish a philosophy of ministry that will meet those needs and plan to grow until it is large enough to conduct that sort of ministry adequately.

---

from week to week, and a choir of 25 seems just right to many church members. Others are more comfortable when Sunday morning is a celebratory event, and several hundred or thousands are present, traffic is congested in the neighborhood, multiple musical groups and orchestras perform and perhaps television cameras are present. If the former is desired, almost any size church can do it. If it is the latter, however, a church of 500 or even 1,000 may not be big enough.

It is recommended that a church carefully examine the needs of the unchurched people around it, establish a philosophy of ministry that will meet those needs and plan to grow until it is large enough to conduct that sort of ministry adequately. None of this is to say that bigger churches are *better* than smaller churches, but they obviously can do many things a smaller church cannot do.

The Celebration, Congregation and Cell

The fourth vital sign could be called the "internal organs" of the Body of Christ. It is the proper balance of the dynamic relationship between celebration, congregation and cell. The way people group themselves together in a church has a lot to do with its growth. Three basic groupings should be considered to find the right balance for a given church in a given situation. The largest is the membership group, which can be almost any size; the middle one is the fellowship group, which should be somewhere around 35 to 80; and the smallest is the spiritual kinship group, which is limited to 8 to 12 persons. I like to call these three structures *celebration, congregation* and *cell.*

Small churches frequently plateau at around 200 members because they have not developed a system for multiplying the number of internal fellowship groups, whether congregations or cells. If new groups are not continually developed, little growth can be expected. Large churches may plateau if their several internal fellowship groups develop individual growth problems, but this difficulty is frequently invisible to the leadership. Lyle Schaller has provided many valuable insights into this vital sign in his writings, for example, pages 69 through 98 in his *Assimilating New Members* (Abingdon Press).

A Common Homogeneous Denominator

The fifth vital sign is that growing churches ordinarily find their memberships are drawn basically from one people group or so-called homogeneous unit. This does not necessarily mean they are racist, or that their doors are closed to anyone from any other group who wants to come to their churches, worship with them or becomes members. It does mean, however, that they offers programs that are meeting the particular spiritual needs of the members of a specific people group, and in no way can one local church do a good job of meeting the needs of all the various people groups.

This has become one of the most controversial principles associated with the Church Growth Movement. It is directly related to two of the diseases we will be discussing later, however, namely ethnikitis (chapter 2) and people-blindness (chapter 4), so I will postpone further comment.

Effective Evangelistic Methods

The sixth vital sign is so obvious that it hardly needs to be mentioned: evangelistic methods that have proven effective in making disciples. By definition, if a church is growing (unless the growth is all biological and transfer growth) something evangelistic must be working. Evangelistic methodologies are so diverse that no one method can be recommended as superior to others. Each church has to develop its own tailor-made method that will bring unbelievers to Christ and then draw them into fellowship with other Christians. Churches that have discovered the most effective methods will grow.

Biblical Priorities

Priorities properly arranged in biblical order constitute the seventh vital sign. This often is strongly influenced by "national institutional factors." That is, some denominational bureaucracies have made strategic decisions on behalf of their constituents that have been definite contributing factors to church decline. In my opinion, prioritizing social ministries over evangelism was the number one contributing factor to denominational membership loss beginning in 1965. This will be discussed again in relationship to the disease called "arrested spiritual development" (chapter 8).

FOUR AXIOMS OF CHURCH GROWTH

Before we move on to examine the specific diseases with which a church may become infected, it will be well to look at four *preconditions* to vigorous church growth. As you will see, they are derived partially from some of the seven vital signs of a healthy church, but their focus is slightly different for they pinpoint the basic essentials. A church can score well on, let's say, as few as four or five of the seven vital signs and perhaps grow if it has an otherwise exceptionally strong growth mix. A church, however, cannot score very low on even one of these four axioms and still expect to grow well.

Axiom 1: The pastor must want the church to grow and be willing to pay the price.

As we hinted earlier in the first vital sign, the pastor is the major key to the growth of the local church. Some may believe certain theological viewpoints that would question whether this is the way things *ought* to be, but research through the years continues to confirm that it is a fact. I have yet to see a growing church in which the pastor does not want the church to grow and is not willing to pay the price.

Doesn't every pastor want his or her church to grow? Sadly, the answer to this is no. Larry Richards once conducted a national survey of 5,000 pastors randomly selected by computer, testing their attitudes about various issues. He found that less than half of the pastors gave high priority to "planning and implementing church growth."

It is true that church growth is onerous to certain people. Some pastors were trained in seminary not to yearn for growth in their ministries. They were taught to believe that "small is beautiful," and that nongrowing churches are more likely to be characterized by superior quality. They say they prefer quality to quantity. Vigorous growth is to be avoided, according to some, because it might distort the true mission of the Church, which is to endure suffering in the midst of a hostile world.

Growth to some can be regarded as undignified. As Howard L. Rice of San Francisco Theological Seminary writes:

> For traditional main-line Protestant denominations the whole subject of confronting the world...with the Good News of Jesus Christ is thought of as unseemly or in poor taste. With relatively few exceptions, the whole matter of winning persons for Christ is viewed as something for the "unwashed" sect groups.[4]

Although some pastors may say they want growth, they may not be willing to pay the price. Church growth does not come cheaply, and therefore not every pastor can handle it. Pastors who wish to count the cost of growth need to consider at least four things:

A. They must be willing to work hard. Pastoring a church that is growing rapidly is much more difficult than pastoring a declining church. A declining church becomes easier to pastor every year! Long hours, large expenditures of energy and a heavy burden of responsibilities await a pastor whose church begins to grow.

B. They must be willing to take the training. Although growth leadership comes intuitively to some who have special spiritual gifts, advanced training in the area of church growth and leadership can make all the difference in the world to most. Few of today's pastors have received systematic instruction in church growth during their years in seminary or Bible school. Excellent training is now available, but it costs money, it takes time and it requires self-discipline.

C. They must be willing to share the ministry. Some pastors are so constituted that they think they must do virtually all the ministry of the church themselves. They have little or no inclination to share leadership in ministry either with professional staff or with the laity. Although nothing may be intrinsically wrong with this, it should be frankly evaluated as a limitation to the growth of the church.

D. They must be willing to include members they cannot pastor personally. In a church of up to 200 members, one pastor can provide fairly adequate attention to the pastoral needs of the whole flock. Beyond that, capacities are stretched, and if vigorous growth continues, in no way can a one-on-one relationship any longer be maintained with all church members. Personal pastoral attention will have to be provided by someone else. This is too high a price for some pastors to pay, so they avoid growth as much as possible.

Axiom 2: The people must want the church to grow and be willing to pay the price.
Although the pastor may be the key person for growth, if the people are not motivated growth will be difficult. After all, the church is neither a building nor an institution; ultimately, it is *people*. Some of my worst experiences come from telephone calls from pastors who have taken church growth training, have gone back to their churches full of enthusiasm, and have been stopped cold by an obstinate board of deacons or a session or a vestry. Frustration levels run high because the pastors know that if they fail to stimulate goal ownership on the part of the lay leaders of the church in one way or another, dreams for church growth cannot be fulfilled.

The price a congregation pays for growth differs somewhat from that of the pastor. It has at least three dimensions:

A. The people must accept the pastor's leadership. In many churches the pastor is not expected to be a leader. A group of lay people have accumulated a certain kind of seniority in the church, and the church, to all intents and purposes, is in their hands and in their control. Pastors come and go. While they are there, they are expected to serve as ecclesiastical housekeepers. They preach sermons, baptize, attend committee meetings, marry the young and bury the dead. Expected pastoral tenure is set at about three to six years by an unwritten but consistently applied by-law. This assures the church fathers and mothers that their control will not be threatened. By so arranging this, they have constructed an effective system for nongrowth.

B. The church members must be willing to provide the funds for growth. Most church growth in America is expensive. I personally see nothing wrong in this. Church members could spend their money on things much less noble than winning their friends and neighbors to Christ. The willingness to give, however, is usually a necessity for growth.

For example, a few years ago my own church, Lake Avenue Congregational Church, decided that a new sanctuary would be necessary to accommodate the growing number of people God has given it in recent years. The price tag came to more than $25 million, which must be contributed by those of us who are members. The rule of thumb was suggested that members should calculate their net worth, and give 10 percent of it during a three-year period, over and above their regular tithes. That was not an easy commitment to make, but no one said that winning people to Christ in Pasadena, California, would be easy. My wife, Doris, and I decided to do our part and trust God for the 10 percent. We now have more money invested in our church building than we do in our private home! Hundreds of other members are doing the same. Result: growth is now a possibility, and the church has continued to grow.

C. They must be willing to sacrifice fellowship for growth. For many church members, this is the most difficult part of the price to pay. When a growing church begins to pass the 100 to 200 mark, more and more strangers are noticed in the worship service. The church is no longer one happy family where everyone knows everyone else. Fellowship has to take place in several subgroups rather than among the membership group as a whole. And, as I have said, if the church is to continue to grow well the fellowship groups have to be prepared to divide regularly. Some people dislike this idea so much they refuse to support goals for growth. If enough refuse, the church simply won't grow.

Axiom 3: The church must agree that the goal of evangelism is to make disciples.

I have seen churches in which the pastor is gung ho for growth, the congregation is in agreement, the budget is available, but still little growth takes place. One reason may be that tne evangelistic program of the church is geared to having people make "decisions for Christ," rather than to becoming responsible disciples. Decisions for Christ are important, but they are only part of the story. Each person who makes a commitment to Christ should also be encouraged to make a simultaneous commitment to the Body of Christ. This, I believe, is soundly biblical. It is also practical and necessary for church growth.

I will go into more detail about this when I describe the disease called "hyper-cooperativism" (see chapter 5).

Axiom 4: The church must not have a terminal illness.

The concept of a church that has a terminal illness has not been widely recognized in Christian circles; but it is an all too common phenomenon. We have no way of knowing how many of the approximately 300,000 Protestant churches in America might have a terminal illness. One recent study, however, showed that between 3 and 6 percent of the 40,000 Southern Baptist churches probably have a terminal disease. If this figure were true nationwide, it would mean that perhaps 18,000 churches are about to expire.

Churches die hard. Many of them go out kicking and screaming, so to speak, and bring little blessing to the kingdom of God in the process. This, however, is not necessary. If churches that have terminal illnesses discover them early enough and face the situation boldly and realistically, they can die with dignity. I once heard Wendell Belew of the Southern Baptist Home Mission Board say, tongue in cheek, that the next department they create ought to be a "Department of

Euthanasia." I didn't know what to think of it at first, but the more I have thought about it, the more I think such a department might become a great asset to God's kingdom.

Churches that have terminal illnesses cannot die with dignity if they do not know what is happening to them. As far as I know, there are two common terminal illnesses, ethnikitis and ghost town disease. The other six diseases are serious, but not necessarily terminal. It is time now to describe them all.

Notes
1. Ted Haggard, *Primary Purpose* (Orlando, Fla.: Creation House, 1995), p. 174.
2. Dean R. Hoge and David A. Roozen, eds., *Understanding Church Growth and Decline 1950-1978* (New York/Philadelphia: The Pilgrim Press, 1979).
3. For example, more than 2,000 pastors have been trained in diagnostic procedures in the Fuller Seminary Doctor of Ministry Program, 135 North Oakland Ave., Pasadena, California 91182.
4. Howard L. Rice, "Foreword," in Foster H. Shannon, *The Growth Crisis in the American Church* (Pasadena, William Carey Library, 1977), p. xii.

Chapter 2

ETHNIKITIS: SHOULD WE MOVE OUR CHURCH?

Ethnikitis is one of the two terminal illnesses of churches. I am listing it first because it is, without peer, the most ruthless killer of churches in America today. One study estimated that among Southern Baptist churches alone, possibly 2,000 were suffering from ethnikitis. At one point in time, more than 50 percent of Southern Baptist churches in Baltimore were diagnosed as having ethnikitis. This is not a disease specific to Southern Baptists, however. Virtually no denomination that has churches in America's cities today has been immune.

Many books focusing on the contemporary religious situation in America recognize the problem of "ethnikitis," although that label is my own invention and other names are also used. It has been called, among other things, "the changing church," "the church in the changing community," "the transitional church" and "the ex-neighborhood church." Some authors are realistic enough to admit that the situation is terminal, but many others stop short of that prognosis. They suggest that the pastors and leaders of such churches can decide to make certain changes that can cure the illness.

TERMINAL ILLNESSES

I realize that the idea that churches, like human beings, can have terminal illnesses is not a popular thought. Warning a church that it is about to die can seem to be a denial of biblical faith and hope. I suppose that medical doctors live with the same dilemma as they weigh the pros and cons of full disclosure to their patients. In my opinion, however, if a church does have a terminal illness such as ethnikitis, the sooner it knows the true state of affairs the better. At the very least, the church can make plans to die with dignity! At the best, its inevitable death can become a blessing to the community in which it is located.

Unfortunately, many churches suffering from ethnikitis do not even know that such a disease exists. Kirk Hadaway, one of America's premier church researchers, agrees that conditions that ordinarily precipitate the disease can readily be discerned well ahead of the time when a crisis might surface. He laments, however: "It always seems to catch churches by surprise."[1]

It is important to recognize the operational difference between *institutional* factors and *contextual* factors. Institutional factors are those that to one degree or another can be controlled by the local church or the denomination in question. That is why church diseases caused by institutional factors are by and large curable illnesses. Contextual factors, however, are sociological factors *beyond the control* of the church. They are similar to earthquakes here in California. Those of us who live in California would rather not have earthquakes, but we can do nothing about it. On the other hand, termites eating our houses are more like institutional factors—we can prevent termite damage if we decide to take the steps to do what is necessary. If the same house is damaged by an earthquake, we cannot attribute it to our personal negligence.

Ethnikitis, like an earthquake, is beyond the control of the local church that contracts it. Once it sets in, the church can and should decide how to react to it appropriately, but the disease itself cannot be reversed. Ethnikitis, I repeat, cannot be traced to local institutional factors, but rather to local contextual factors.

As soon as I say that the disease cannot be reversed, I need to qualify the statement. God can and still does do miracles. AIDS, for example, is a deadly illness; but cases have been reported in which AIDS has been cured by the miraculous power of God. Not many, however. The general rule is that AIDS patients, even in Assemblies of God churches where prayer for the sick is high profile, die. The same is true of ethnikitis and also of ghost town disease, which will be explained in the next chapter. Some churches have been healed from these diseases and have moved into renewed growth patterns, but they are few and far between. The general rule is that they die.

Because ethnikitis is caused by contextual factors, it is probably more helpful to focus attention on the changing *community* rather than the changing *church*. As we shall see, the problem usually revolves around a static church in a changing neighborhood.

THE SCENARIO

The scenario precipitating church ethnikitis is familiar to most families who have lived in urban areas in the United States. The church that contracts ethnikitis was once a *neighborhood church*. It was started to reach out and meet the needs of one basic kind of people, namely those who had been living in the specific neighborhood in which the church was planted. The church then grew and often flourished because the people living in the neighborhood were attracted to that particular congregation. The unchurched typically perceived the church members as "our kind of people." Their language, their worship styles, their musical tastes, their social activities and their personal lifestyles were compatible.

Some urban churches are not neighborhood churches. Usually in the downtown area many "old first churches" were established sometimes generations ago as the major outpost of a given denomination in the city. Others are "metropolitan regional churches," which draw their constituency from many scattered parts of the metropolitan area. These kinds of churches are not particularly susceptible to ethnikitis, although from time to time cases have been recorded.

In the case of many neighborhood churches, an unanticipated and unprayed-for social phenomenon often begins to occur. Other kinds of people begin moving into the neighborhood—perhaps just a few at first, then in greater numbers.

They predictably enjoy the company of one another more than that of the people who have been born and raised in the neighborhood. Some of the behavior of the newcomers seems strange to the long-term residents. It is harder to make friends with them. Their children sometimes don't get along too well with the children of the church members. Gradually church families begin moving out of the changing neighborhood and into new neighborhoods in which their own values and lifestyles are more readily accepted.

The families who move out, however, usually remain loyal to the church. They have formed close friendships there, they have invested considerable money in the building and program, and they feel at home there on Sundays, even though they no longer want to be in their old neighborhood the rest of the week. Therefore, many of them commute to the church for weekly services and maintain active membership.

The Church Becomes an Island

As this process continues, sometimes quite rapidly and sometimes more slowly, the result is a church that is virtually an island of one kind of people, in the midst of a community of another kind of people, and very little communication between the two. Such a church has contracted what we call "ethnikitis." It begins to decline, first of all, because the people in the neighborhood are no longer being won into their neighborhood church. Furthermore, even if the members who have moved away are evangelistically inclined and winning some of their new neighbors to Christ, there is little chance that these new converts will want to commute with them back to their old church. The new converts generally believe they will be better served by the churches in their own neighborhood.

Churches that contract ethnikitis can die in as short a period as 5 years or less, depending on the rapidity of the population change and the cultural distance between the groups involved. Others may survive for 15 or 20 years. The crunch ordinarily comes when the children of those who have moved away reach elementary school age. At this point in life, the parents often stop commuting to their old church and join a church where their children will enjoy a Sunday School and church life more in harmony with their day-to-day school situation.

Meanwhile, older members whose children are no longer at

home will frequently continue in the church. Some will commute to the worship services, and others may have remained in the old neighborhood because they could not afford to move away. In any case, the age profile of the congregation continues to climb, and the death rate among them continues to increase. By then, gloom and despair have usually begun. The church is no longer the happy, joy-filled place it used to be.

AN EPIDEMIC OF ETHNIKITIS

All too many real-life illustrations of ethnikitis can be found. For example, a severe epidemic of ethnikitis that swept Southern Baptist churches in Birmingham, Alabama, was one that has been documented and recorded. Between 1966 and 1973, a rapid population shift took place in Birmingham as a result of new conditions created by the civil rights movement sweeping America in those days. Blacks began moving into formerly all-white neighborhoods.

The Baptist *Home Missions* magazine boldly published a dramatic two-page spread, showing eight graphs of church decline, each one superimposed over a ghostlike photograph of the church facility as it used to be. Of the eight churches that died, seven of them died of ethnikitis. The eighth was a fairly new church plant, which we might say happened to be stillborn. And the article went on to warn that 42 more Baptist churches in Birmingham might soon be faced with ethnikitis.

The population change in Birmingham was so radical that three of the churches died in four years. None of them lasted for more than eight years after ethnikitis first started. At their high points, the eight churches had a cumulative Sunday School enrollment of more than 3,000, so the net loss was substantial. I am not aware of the exact conditions in which all the churches died. At least one, Calvary Baptist Church, died with dignity and had a happy celebration when they turned their facilities over to the black Thirteenth Avenue Macedonian Baptist Church.[2]

AUSTIN CONGREGATIONAL CHURCH

A fascinating analysis of a classic case of ethnikitis is presented by Walter Ziegenhals of the Community Renewal Society of Chicago. It concerns Austin Congregational Church, built in the 1920s in the Austin suburb of Chicago, which at that time was a pleasant, quiet, well-scrubbed place for white, upper-middle class families. The church, which was built by the first generation of members, fit their tastes well. It included a gymnasium, a Moeller pipe organ and living quarters for the custodian. Its outreach program was effective, and, in a period of 30 years, Austin Congregational Church grew steadily to more than 500 members.

In 1950, however, ethnikitis developed. Ziegenhals says:

> The next 20 years weave a sad and familiar tale of inevitable decline. Older members of the church retire or move away or die. Younger families move to the suburbs. Blacks begin to move into Austin. Community leaders offer sober and reasoned pronouncements about the importance of an integrated community. By 1966 the power structure was accused of fleeing to the suburbs and of not "giving a damn" about Austin Church.[3]

Here is a clear case of a church going out kicking and screaming instead of dying with dignity. When Christian people start swearing at one another, something is seriously wrong. The Austin church had been suffering from a terminal illness for several years, but the congregation was unable to cope with it realistically enough to die with dignity. Ziegenhals summarizes the basic principle:

> The history of Austin Church reveals once again that we are not going to be blessed with integrated churches, at least not in the foreseeable future. In communities like Hyde Park, where the University of Chicago generates a continuing supply of whites, that possibility still exists. Changing communities like Austin offer no such hope. The exodus of whites, like the corresponding influx of blacks, is inexorable.[4]

On the bright side, the story of Austin Church does have a happy ending, but I will save that for later.

The examples of Birmingham and Austin both involve African-Americans moving into predominantly white neighborhoods. That population shift has undoubtedly been the most frequent cause of ethnikitis in American cities today. The same thing has happened when large numbers of Hispanics have moved into both black neighborhoods and into Anglo neighborhoods or when Koreans have moved into African-American neighborhoods. It should be noted, however, that racial population changes such as these are not the only causes of ethnikitis. Even when race is constant, changes in social class can equally affect church growth. Let me provide an example.

AFRICAN-AMERICAN ETHNIKITIS

I know, for example, of a black church in a black neighborhood that has contracted a form of ethnikitis. The problem in this case is not rooted in a change in the community, which has remained relatively stable, but rather in a change in certain families living in the community. This is the outworking of a very important church growth principle described by renowned missiologist, Donald McGavran, as "redemption and lift." Here is how it happened in this particular church.

The church was started by a popular African-American preacher in a black community. The Lord blessed his efforts and brought hundreds of people to Christ and to the church through his ministry. The community itself was fairly poor, as American communities go. When men and women found new life in Jesus Christ, however, not only did they find hope for life eternal, but things also began to change in their lives then and there. Broken marriages were restored. Drunkenness, brawling and immorality were reduced. Children were loved more. Employers found they had more faithful and efficient employees. Family budgets stabilized, and pay raises came one after the other. The Christians could afford to give more to the church, and a fine sanctuary was built and packed, Sunday after Sunday.

The Christians could afford to give more to their church, and did, and they could also afford better automobiles and better homes. Many of them therefore decided to leave their low-cost housing and move to other neighborhoods, some black and some integrated, where they could develop their new lifestyles with maximum freedom. Because they recognized that their relationship to Jesus Christ had a great deal to do with their social lift, they remained fiercely loyal to their church, and commuted long distances to be there every Sunday. The process happened gradually, and because no

---

Although seeking cures for ethnikitis might be fruitless, nevertheless, developing solutions for the problem at hand may enable the church to die with dignity.

---

racial difference was involved, they were not accused of indulging in "black flight" or of "not giving a damn" about their neighborhood.

Nevertheless, the church began a steady decline. The upwardly mobile blacks in the church began to lose meaningful contact and communication with the poorer blacks who moved into the housing they had vacated. Those in the neighborhood undoubtedly looked with envy at the array of shiny Cadillacs and Lincolns and Oldsmobiles in the church parking lot on Sunday mornings. No longer were the people of the church winning the lost who were living near the church and bringing them into their fellowship as they had done in previous years. The church is now only half full, and the decline will in all probability continue until the church finally dies. It has contracted ethnikitis.

WHAT IS THE SOLUTION?

Terminal illnesses, by definition, are incurable, short of a miraculous work of God. Although it is never wrong to pray that God will intervene, in most cases it would be both unrealistic and presumptuous to plan for the future on the assumption that God will come to the rescue. Although seeking *cures* for ethnikitis might be fruitless, nevertheless, developing *solutions* for the problem at hand may enable the church to die with dignity. With one possible exception, which I will mention later, ethnikitis has no known cure. If it did, I would be the first to recommend it. Instead I see four options for attempting to deal with an unfortunate problem. I will list the four plus the one exception from what I believe is the least advisable to the most advisable.

1. *Die a lingering death.* This is the option that many churches choose when either they refuse to recognize what is happening to them, or when they recognize it but do nothing about it. Most churches infected with ethnikitis go this route. Lyle Schaller, a church consultant, calls it "hanging on until you have to die," and he agrees with me that it is the least rational way of dealing with problems caused by a transitional urban community.

For example, I vividly recall talking to the elders of a Presbyterian church many years ago and explaining to them that they were well into the process of dying from ethnikitis (although at that time the word had not yet been coined). I was telling them something they didn't want to hear so they became upset with me. They were so deeply into a state of denial that some of their rejoinders bordered on calling into question my standards of Christian social ethics. My impression was that they thought I was talking through my hat. In less than five years, however, the church closed its doors. The vacant building later became a community center unrelated to preaching the gospel, and soon after that it caught fire and burned to the ground!

There must have been a better way to do it!

2. *Adopt a "social mission" philosophy of ministry.* The usual situation in a neighborhood that is causing a church to have ethnikitis is that the new people who move in find themselves at a lower socioeconomic level than those attending the church. This is not the case with the phenomenon of the newer urban "gentrification" taking place, but that is still a fairly rare exception to the rule. In some cases, the new people are definitely hurting, experiencing acute problems of unemployment, marital instability, inadequate housing, lack of legal and

medical services, dysfunctional families, need for recreational facilities, high crime rates and hunger.

Christian compassion, arising from Christ's command to "love your neighbor as yourself," opens believers' hearts to want to help those around them as much as possible. Although the new people in the community may not be inclined to receive the gospel or to join a church predominantly composed of a kind of people with whom they have little in common culturally, they will nevertheless be grateful for any kind of social help that can alleviate their immediate situation.

Some churches, recognizing that they have ethnikitis, decide to use their remaining human and financial resources to minister to the social needs of the neighborhood. Many experiments with this option have shown that becoming a social mission will not ordinarily stem the decline in church membership, and the church eventually will die. That is why the social mission philosophy of ministry is not listed as a cure. Showing compassion for the poor, however, is one of the ways of dying with dignity and ministering in the name of the Lord. The church will be remembered as being a blessing to the community, and God will be glorified.

3. *Attempt a conglomerate church.* Many church leaders, aware that in the kingdom of God barriers of race and culture and social class should not divide believers, desire their congregations to mix people from various cultures in worship, fellowship and ministry. Intuitively they say, "If we as individuals and as a congregation are characterized by the fruit of the Holy Spirit, there is no limit to the variety of cultures and lifestyles we can have living in harmony in the same congregation. If we can solve the spiritual problems, the social problems will take care of themselves." They believe they can cure ethnikitis by engineering changes in attitudes and ministry styles.

This would, by far, be the most ideal way to handle church ethnikitis. A few experiments in developing conglomerate churches have succeeded. I think of churches such as the Church on Brady, a Southern Baptist Church in East Los Angeles, California, led by Tom Wolfe. I think of Jubilee Christian Center, a new apostolic church in San Jose, California, led by Dick Bernal. Others could be added to the list, but when all is said and done, the list would still be much shorter than we might like.

Realistically speaking, the odds of success for a conglomerate church are so low that I include it in this list of options somewhat reluctantly. I know of many pastors who invested deeply in such efforts, only to find that their subsequent failures led to critical setbacks in their personal lives and their ministries, and I hesitate to do or say anything that would tend to add to their number. Although I, therefore, do not recommend this approach to most pastors whose churches are experiencing ethnikitis, I nevertheless would recommend it to some. Who are these "some"?

The major variable that separates the few successful conglomerate churches from the many failures is a senior pastor who has the missionary gift. As those familiar with my book *Your Spiritual Gifts Can Help Your Church Grow* (Regal Books) would know, the spiritual gift of missionary is the ability to minister in a second culture with whatever other gifts a person might have. My research regarding the frequency of the missionary gift leads me to believe that about 1 percent of the members of the Body of Christ have been given this gift by God. This number applies to pastors as well as to laypeople.

The upshot is that most pastors, whether Anglo or Korean or African-American or Hispanic or Chinese, are monocultural. They may be highly effective among their own people group, but the farther they get from it, culturally speaking, the more their ministry effectiveness is diminished. Because spiritual gifts are distributed at God's discretion (see 1 Cor. 12:11,18), feelings of inadequacy or guilt on the part of the pastor are uncalled for. Realistic self-evaluation or "thinking soberly of oneself," to paraphrase Romans 12:3, is always a good idea. Pastors who know their limitations, in this case their cultural limitations, have a great advantage over colleagues who persist in a state of denial.

4. *Move out.* Moving the church out of the neighborhood that has now changed, and into a new neighborhood where once again the evangelistic responsibilities of the church can be fulfilled, makes good sense. It opens the way for further church growth and for new men and women to find the Savior and be reconciled to God. Many churches experiencing ethnikitis select this option. As a matter of fact, this is usually the

most positive and feasible solution to the problem of ethnikitis. The downside is that the church may be criticized by those who have chosen other options as yielding to the temptation of "white flight," if in fact the church that relocates is an Anglo church.

The option of moving out of the neighborhood can be exercised in two ways—through merger or through relocation. The congregation can decide to move as a group and join

---

Making a clean transition
by changing the existing church
into a church more relevant to the
new community is the best way
to die with dignity.

---

forces with an existing church in the new neighborhood. If this is being considered, church leaders should be aware of the usual mathematics of merger: $1 + 1 = 1$! Merger has not proved to be a formula for church growth.

If the church chooses to maintain its congregational identity and acquire a new meeting place of its own in a more favorable location, the future growth potential is higher. Now suppose this is done and the congregation relocates and begins to grow again. Might it not be said that the church did not actually die? In one way a church is not a *building,* it is *people,* and therefore a congregation that leaves one sanctuary and enters another does not die. This is true from the viewpoint of the congregation, but think of it from the viewpoint of the old neighborhood. As far as the old neighborhood is concerned, the church that used to be there is now dead and gone. The ethnikitis was terminal.

Whether understood as renewal or death, from both legitimate viewpoints, relocation is in many cases the most realistic way of solving ethnikitis.

THE BEST SOLUTION OF ALL

5. Make a transition. In my opinion, making a clean transition by changing the existing church into a church more relevant to the new community is the best way to die with dignity. It can be likened to a complete blood transfusion—get rid of the old blood and introduce new blood.

This process is not easy. Although it is the most recommended solution, it is also the most difficult. Tom Roote, a Baptist executive who was working with churches in Birmingham during the epidemic of ethnikitis I previously described, agrees that "it is difficult for churches to acknowledge that they may have to go out of business." He tells of one pastor who had an inkling that his church might be terminally infected, so Roote suggested they plan to close the church. Roote says, "He just couldn't bring himself to do it. We're success-oriented in business, in every area; that's churches, too."[5]

Some object to this option on theological or ethical grounds. They believe that rather than make transitions, the congregation should integrate with the people moving into the community, inviting them to become members of their church. Although such an approach certainly does have sterling theological and ethical justification, it does not work in the great majority of cases. For some time, particularly through the 1960s, it was being experimented with widely and the jury was still undecided. The jury is now in, however, and the verdict is not too positive. The attempt to force local church integration of differing people groups has been losing strength, including among church leaders on the liberal side of the fence who have advocated it most strongly in the past. An editorial in *Christian Century,* a liberal magazine, for example, says:

> Major Protestant denominations are coming to realize that if they are going to continue to have a presence in the city, it will be in the form of black or Hispanic churches. In the 50s and early 60s the "integrated church" was widely viewed as an embodiment of the ideal of Christian unity, one that was worth seeking and possible to achieve. In the 70s sober realism has set in, and the "integrated church" that goes beyond tokenism is seen as a

very temporary fixture on the religious land-
scapes—a "church in transition" from white to
non-white.[6]

A HAPPY ENDING

Back now to Austin Congregational Church. It died in 1969,
but I mentioned earlier that the story has a happy ending. In
1973, four years after the doors of the church were closed, its
denomination, the United Church of Christ (UCC), decided to
participate in a formal agreement with a large black Baptist
church. Walter Ziegenhals says it should have been done at
least 2 years earlier. In my opinion, it probably should have
been done 8 to 10 years earlier, particularly when the
Christians in the church started swearing at each other. But
better late than never!

Together the Congregationalists and the Baptists decided to
form a new African-American congregation called the Austin
Baptist United Church of Christ. The UCC would provide the
building and the finances. The Baptists would provide an
experienced black pastor and a nucleus of 10 laypeople.
Within three years, the tiny nucleus had grown to a membership of 160 having an average of 70 in attendance at Sunday
morning worship. This is excellent church growth. Once again
Austin Church, this time in a completely new style, format
and cultural environment, is ministering to and attracting
neighborhood people to a neighborhood congregation.

MAKING THE TRANSITION

Because considering the option of making an ethnic transition
is at once both desirable and difficult, it would be well to
explain what is involved. Let's use a typical transition from a
predominantly Anglo congregation to a predominantly
African-American congregation as an example.

As I see the transition process, it ordinarily would be initiated by the white congregation that has been located in the neighborhood long before it actually dies. This is similar to a human
being taking the precaution of preparing a will instead of having the heirs settle the estate, as did Austin Congregational
Church so to speak. Definite plans should be agreed upon by

the parties involved to finalize the transition by a specified date. As a missiologist, I can easily see this process being parallel to "indigenizing" the church, as we say, or transferring it to the nationals on the foreign mission field. In this case, the role of the "missionaries" is being played by the white church leaders, and the "nationals" are represented by the African-Americans who are moving into the neighborhood.

One year or so before the transition date, a black copastor should be hired. If a nucleus of laypeople can come along, all the better. The evangelistic outreach thrust for the year should focus on the new residents in the community, members of the people group who will be responsible for sustaining the church long range. For prayer and for personal motivation, the percentages of newcomers and old-timers should be calculated and constantly communicated to the congregation. Throughout the process, the whites must be saying with heartfelt enthusiasm: "We must decrease while they must increase!" Whether African-Americans are by then a majority or not, the agreed-upon date for transition should be faithfully kept and a celebration service should be held to bring closure.

At that time, the white copastor resigns and moves on. All white church officers resign and black church officers are installed. The day-by-day membership can and probably should continue to be integrated for as long as possible, but not the *leadership*, for at least two years. At the end of two years, any remaining white members should be once again considered eligible for election or appointment to church office. By this time, if they are elected, the situation will be different. They will find themselves as minority white officers of a majority black church.

I realize that this solution may sound drastic to some. It requires a higher-than-average trust in the Holy Spirit and His ability to work through the new people for the glory of God. It demands a level of humility many Christians would not be willing to display. The tendency of many is to be chicken-hearted and continue to stretch out the process, postponing the date set for closure. I do not recommend it. We are talking about major surgery, and, in my opinion, the sooner it is performed the better. The more complete the blood transfusion, the higher will be the future evangelistic potential of the church in the new community.

An outstanding example of a transition occurred in Kansas City, Missouri, several years ago. Trinity Baptist Church, a white Southern Baptist congregation, was afflicted with a severe case of ethnikitis. Blacks were rapidly moving into the neighborhood, and the resultant "white flight" from the community was occurring with a vengeance. Trinity Baptist, realizing that its days were numbered, wisely decided to die with dignity. Its membership had by that time become so scattered in the suburbs that it had little chance of a successful relocation, so the congregation decided to dissolve. When it did, it *donated* its attractive $175,000 building to a struggling African-American congregation, Spruce St. Matthews Baptist Church, and no strings attached. In less than two years, attendance at Spruce St. Matthews rose from 100 to 500. Outstanding church growth! The death of Trinity became a blessing to the kingdom of God.

A teaching about this kind of death with dignity is taught in the Bible. Jesus said, "Unless a grain of wheat falls into the earth and dies, it remains alone; but if it dies, it bears much fruit" (John 12:24, *RSV*).

IMMIGRANT CHURCHES

Before leaving the discussion of ethnikitis, a related problem that is not exactly ethnikitis, but that perhaps we could call "maladaptation," needs to be mentioned. Many churches, brought to America by certain groups of immigrants, have experienced serious growth problems after 30 to 50 years of reasonably good health. The Evangelical Covenant Church, the North American Baptists, the Moravians, the Reformed Church in America, the Baptist General Conference, the Lutheran Church Missouri Synod and many others have developed specific growth problems directly related to their ethnic origins. Some denominations, such as the United Methodists, the Southern Baptists, the Pentecostal Holiness and the National Baptists, to name a few, do not have these kinds of problems.

The Evangelical Covenant Church used to be the Swedish Covenant Church. The North American Baptists used to be the German Baptists. The Reformed Church in America used to be the Dutch Reformed Church, and so forth. These churches enjoyed growth in America as long as an ongoing supply of immigrant people came who had similar ethnic roots. The people arriving in America perceived those churches to be "our kind of people," and in them they could readily hear and accept the message of Jesus Christ. Beyond that, they welcomed the social contact with people who shared their lifestyles and values. For their children, the churches afforded an excellent marriage market.

Immigration patterns, however, shift. Swedish, German and Dutch people are relatively meltable in American society. Give them a few generations, and they are ordinarily assimilated into the mainstream Anglo-American culture. They no longer feel the same need for ethnic-oriented churches, and as time goes by they are repulsed by them. To the extent that the church retains its Swedishness or its Germanness or its Dutchness, it will therefore eventually decline because newer immigrants in America today are predominantly from non-European races representing more radically distinct cultures. Hispanics, Koreans, Filipinos, French and Arabs are not nearly as meltable into the Anglo-American culture as were the northern and western Europeans who dominated our former immigration patterns.

Churches that have remained ethnic too long, and are experiencing growth problems as a result, are not terminal. It would be inaccurate to say they have ethnikitis. They simply need to take the necessary steps to adapt to American culture and become Anglo-American churches, in most cases.

An outstanding example of accomplishing this is a well-known Reformed Church in the United States that is located in Orange County, California, although many people, including some members, would have no idea that it is a Reformed Church. Its founding pastor, Robert Schuller, is pedigreed Dutch, and not only was born of the "right" parents, but also attended the "right" schools, and married the "right" woman. When Robert Schuller was assigned the task of planting a new church in Orange County about 20 years ago, he conducted a demographic study and discovered that few Dutch people lived in the vicinity. So Pastor Schuller decided to call the church Garden Grove Community Church and relegate the Reformed Church in America to a footnote in the church bulletin. It grew vigorously and later became known as the

Crystal Cathedral. It is still a Reformed Church, but most of its members couldn't care less about Calvin's *Institutes* or the Synod of Dort.

Predictably, Robert Schuller received severe criticism for many years from members of his own denomination. Although saddened by their lack of understanding, he weathered the problems and has been a great blessing to tens of thousands through his church and his television ministry *The Hour of Power*. If someone other than Robert Schuller had come along and insisted on starting a more typically Dutch church in Orange County, the pastor might well be struggling today with a congregation of 150, gaining perhaps two or three new families a year, if that.

Growing churches authentically reflect the culture of the community in which God has placed them. Churches that experience cases of maladaptation need to take action to shed immigrant trappings and become more American, if they desire to grow and win new people to Christ.

Notes
1. C. Kirk Hadaway, ed. Larry L. Rose and C. Kirk Hadaway, "The Church in the Urban Setting," *The Urban Challenge* (Nashville: Broadman Press, 1982), p. 85.
2. Elaine Furlow, "Choices Amid Changes?" *Home Missions* (September 1975): 34-36.
3. Walter E. Ziegenhals, "Austin's 'New' Church," *The Christian Ministry* (November 1976): 5.
4. Ibid., p. 7.
5. Personal conversation with Peter Wagner, n.d.
6. "UCC's Covenants for Churches in Change," *Christian Century* (November 16, 1977): 1055.

Chapter 3

GHOST TOWN DISEASE: EVERYBODY'S LEAVING!

Ghost town disease joins ethnikitis as the two decidedly terminal illnesses of churches. They happen to be the only two of the nine diseases explained in this book that are caused by *contextual* as opposed to *institutional* factors. As a reminder, contextual factors are sociological factors the church cannot control, and institutional factors do fall within the possibility of being controlled or corrected by churches and their leaders.

The immediate implication of such an awareness is that pastors whose churches find themselves afflicted with diseases brought on by contextual factors should not feel guilty or directly responsible for the malady and the resultant decline in church membership. They may rightly assume a primary responsibility for some of the other diseases caused by institutional factors, but not for either ethnikitis or ghost town disease. In these cases, nothing the pastors could have done could have prevented the onset of the unfortunate situations in which they find themselves.

A DETERIORATING COMMUNITY

The underlying cause of ghost town disease is a *deteriorating* community. This differs from ethnikitis, which is caused by a *changing* community. In the case of ethnikitis, old people are moving away from the community and new people are moving in. In the case of ghost town disease, old people are moving out but no one is moving in.

Although ethnikitis is most generally an *urban* phenomenon, ghost town disease is most generally a *rural* phenomenon.

If you have lived for a considerable time in a rural area, you know what this ordinarily looks and feels like. Local schools close and merge to form unified school districts. Bus trips to school become longer and longer. Children leave for college, marry, find jobs, and return, at best, only for Thanksgiving and Christmas. A doctor is more difficult to find than it used to be. The following are some typical quotes from a newspaper article in a midwestern town under the headline, "Small Town Mid-America on Endangered List":

- Notices taped on plate-glass storefronts announce the sales of farms and farm equipment.
- Karen's Cafe is "Closed until May."
- The building that housed the only Chevrolet dealer for miles around is empty. The windows reveal a showroom floor littered with paper and one dead sparrow.
- The town's bank failed last year.
- The collapse of family farms is hurting churches too. An agricultural economist conducted a seminar for rural pastors recently and "learned that there was not a single small-town church that wasn't in economic trouble."
- The economist concluded, "These churches, and social institutions like garden clubs and women's clubs, are doomed to disappear."

By this we are not to imagine that *all* churches in America's small rural towns are or ever will be suffering from ghost town disease. A significant enough number, however, are. A few years ago, for example, Southern Baptist researchers estimated that about 9,000 of their churches were affected by the farm crisis, and of them about 2,000 were classified as *critical*, meaning, I would surmise, that they probably have terminal ghost town disease. In one of the best books available about the rural church, Edward Hassinger, John Holik and Kenneth Benson estimate that about 10 percent of churches in communities less than 2,500 would be suffering from what I am calling "ghost town disease."[1]

CAN CHURCHES DIE OF OLD AGE?

Ghost town disease, more than any of the others, is best seen as having a natural cause. The best human analogy I can think of is old age. People who live into their 70s or 80s are

---

The secret of success for churches is to find a need and fill it, or find a hurt and heal it.

---

expected to become progressively weaker and eventually pass away. Their deaths are painful to family and friends, but not nearly as painful as they would have been if they had been killed in their 40s or 50s by automobile accidents or lung cancer.

Can death come "naturally" to a church? Yes. Ghost town disease, as I see it, leads to what can best be understood as a natural church death. It is regretful, but not necessarily tragic.

SENIOR CITIZENS

Drawing an analogy to old age must not lead us to suppose that an advanced age level among the church members is necessarily a cause of church decline or death. It is true that in the vast majority of churches that are dying of ghost town disease the age profile would be higher than average. The percentage of senior citizens in a congregation, however, is more likely a *symptom* of the disease, not a cause. Some churches composed primarily or entirely of senior citizens are not ill at all—they show superb vitality. For example, a United Methodist church in a Southern California community called Leisure World is healthy and vigorous. It is meeting people's needs and growing. Because no one under 52 is allowed to live in Leisure World, no one under 52 belongs to the church.

If I may be permitted a brief digression, in my opinion the number of churches built on programs designed specifically for senior citizens urgently needs to be multiplied in many parts of the United States today. Demographic studies have been telling us for some time that the quantity of people of retirement age is increasing in a dramatic manner. Plans need to be implemented now, not only in the church, but also in all segments of society, to cope with these changing conditions. This is true now, but it will be more so when the baby boomers reach retirement age.

Many senior citizens are being well cared for in existing churches that embrace the entire age span of society. We must face the fact, however, that an even greater number of senior citizens are not, and, if present circumstances persist, *will* not be touched by existing churches. I believe that large numbers of them could be won, however, by new churches that are geared specifically to meet their needs.

This special kind of church needs to provide, first of all, pastoral leadership uniquely equipped for the task. In most cases it requires a mature person as a leader. The worship style, the hours of services, the social activities, the music, the evangelistic program and all other activities should be tailor-made for older people.

Two common myths need to be dispelled if the doors for more effective senior-specific ministries are to open. The first is the myth that older people are anxious to spend a lot of time with younger people. Occasional contact and a smattering of mixed social events, yes. A steady diet, no. The second is the myth that older people cannot easily be won to Christ. Any person who has needs that Jesus can meet can be won to Christ, and senior citizens in America have more than their share of such needs.

A senior citizens' church can grow. The secret of success for churches, Robert Schuller says, is to find a need and fill it, or find a hurt and heal it. Literally millions of senior citizens in America are hurting and can be won to Christ by churches that specialize in ministry to them.

DIAGNOSING GHOST TOWN DISEASE

As I have said, ghost town disease is more of a *community* problem than a *church* problem, although it affects the church just as it affects businesses, schools, public services, housing and other community institutions.

When rural towns and villages, most of which have churches in them, begin to diminish and eventually disappear, a church has little chance of growing in any of the three ways churches ordinarily add members—biological, transfer or conversion growth.

Such churches cannot grow biologically because the children of the believers do not stay in town as they used to do. Most rural people can remember when grandparents and grandchildren were all attending church together. No longer does this happen.

Churches in diminishing communities cannot depend on transfer growth because not many Christian people carrying letters of transfer to a new church are moving into these towns. How about transfer from other churches in town? Unlike the situation found in many cities, current church members in rural areas have typically developed fierce loyalty to their own churches, and are not prone to church hop, supposing that the grass may be greener on the other side of the fence.

How about conversion growth? The possibilities are slim because many of our declining rural towns are adequately churched, and relatively few unchurched people remain to respond to the gospel. By this, I do not mean that churches in deteriorating communities should back off in the slightest from efforts to share the gospel and convert unbelievers in their communities.

I like the way Kent Hunter puts it: "The shrinking church may be able to win to Jesus Christ people who have never been receptive before. Adversity often stimulates openness to the gospel. Unchurched members of the community are good prospects for the gospel as it is presented in the context of a genuine ministry to their needs."[2] At the same time, I am try-ing to be realistic. Churches in declining rural communities that experience a sustained turnaround as a result of aggres-sive evangelism will still be few and far between

THE CEGO CHURCH

Let's look at a classic case of ghost town disease. This one comes from Cego, Texas, a community so small that I still have not been able to find it on a road map of the Lone Star State.

The town of Cego was founded a generation ago by a group of 100 German immigrant farmers. They had no desire to assimilate into the Anglo-American culture, so they set up their own community 30 miles away from the nearest town. They maintained their old-country customs and developed a self-contained agricultural system. Each family had a few acres they farmed by hand. They grew their own vegetables, raised their own animals for meat, and produced their own milk, cheese and eggs. They sold a few melons nearby for the little cash their simple lifestyle required.

The German farmers were good Christians. They planted a new church when they established Cego. My friend Paul Rutledge, who told me of this interesting case of ghost town disease, pastored their church for two years while he was a student in seminary. At first it had been a United Church of Christ. Then they called a Brethren pastor, so they changed the name to the Brethren Church. Later a Methodist pastor came, and it became a Methodist church. Finally they settled on the name "Cego Church," so they could then call any pastor with-out changing the name again. My friend happened to be a Southern Baptist.

When Paul Rutledge arrived, he discovered that only two people in Cego were not church members. As a good Southern Baptist preacher, however, he took that evangelistic challenge seriously, and before he left he had led one of them to the Lord. His record of reducing the unchurched population of a whole town by 50 percent during a short pastorate is a world record, as far as I know!

All the women of Cego had borne children, but every one of them had moved away to attend school or to get jobs else-where. None of them had returned to the village of their birth to establish residence. New people found nothing in Cego to attract them, so no one moved in either. This eliminated possibilities of biological, transfer or conversion growth, except for the one incorrigible sinner who would not respond to the gospel. When the older people died or became so disabled that they could not farm any longer, their land was bought by the big farmers in the area.

It is clear that the Cego Church has a case of ghost town disease. It may survive for a time, then it will surely die.

SHOULD WE PULL THE PLUG?

Marissa, Illinois, has a population of 2,464, so it is considerably larger than Cego, Texas. Whether or not Marissa is disintegrating I do not know, but the interesting story of Zion United Methodist Church located there bears telling in the context of ghost town disease. It raises an issue that virtually any church having a terminal illness will inevitably face.

Zion Church, founded in 1868, had only three members remaining on its membership list when I first learned about it several years ago. Alex Wildy, 83, and his sister Pearl, 87, were keeping the church open week after week. It was their mother's dying wish that they do so. At each service, flowers were faithfully placed on their mother's grave.

R. David Reynolds was serving as part-time pastor of Zion Church. He pastored another United Methodist church in Marissa as well. Each week Alex Wildy paid the pastor's salary in cash. Wildy himself took charge of lighting the church's kerosene lamps and stoking the coal stove during the winter months.[3]

Although it doesn't supply the answer, the situation at Zion at least raises a question that perhaps many other churches should face realistically. Is this a case of the excessive use of life-support systems? Death is not a disgrace either for a human being or for a church.

Zion United Methodist Church is now closed. As would be expected, Alex Wildy died and is now with the Lord. However, there may have been more wisdom than at first would have been apparent in the decision of the Methodist district to keep the church open that long. In his will, Alex Wildy left $1.5 million to McKindrick Methodist College!

MEETING THE NEEDS
OF DYING CHURCHES

Dying churches, like dying people, have special needs that must be met. One of the most fascinating and insightful discussions of the pastoral care required by dying churches comes from William Willimon, a professor at Duke University Divinity School. At one point in his ministry, Willimon had two assignments. He was simultaneously chaplain in a geriatric hospital and pastor of a church that experienced ghost town disease. His background and training had prepared him to cope with the situation of the people he was counseling, but not the church he was pastoring.

Pastor Willimon became frustrated with his church. It had 50 remaining members, and he began to believe that the only possible reasons for the church's continuing existence must have been to maintain the church's cemetery and to wait for the members either to die or to move away. Every year the budget had to be cut. The members spent a great deal of their energy trying to find somewhere to lay the blame for their decline and in dreaming for some turn of events that would reinstate the "good old days." This was not what Willimon had been taught to expect from a church. He had been programmed to demand growth and change.

One day it occurred to him that his attitudes toward the two institutions he served were inconsistent. When a 90-year-old person in the hospital died a quiet death, neither he nor the physician felt a sense of failure. They were confident they had done everything possible to make the patient physically comfortable and emotionally and spiritually adjusted to accept the inevitable moment of death. Why should he not approach a dying church in the same way? Willimon observes,

> Dying patients may want and need hope, encouragement, absolution, prayer, counseling, hand holding, confession, or a wide variety of pastoral acts. They usually never need the fostering of guilt for their condition or false hopes, scolding, etc.[4]

If these are the needs of people who have terminal illnesses, what might churches that have terminal illnesses require?

I will highlight three felt needs of churches experiencing ghost town disease. Naturally, they are different from the ordinary priority needs of healthy churches, but they are no less important, it seems to me, in the total well-being of the kingdom of God.

1. Guilt Removal

Undoubtedly, the most debilitating symptom a church experiencing terminal ghost town disease might develop is guilt. It is not difficult to see how this could happen. Our American culture is success oriented. Success for churches has ordinarily been defined, at least partially, as growth. Church growth as a corollary of good church health has been a major theme of persons identifying with the Church Growth Movement, me included.

I now believe that we may have been somewhat hasty in our generalization that *any* church can grow if it only *wants* to grow. We need to introduce an escape clause into the general principle that faithfulness to God invariably results in church growth. We should admit that though this may be true of most churches, it does not apply across the board to churches experiencing terminal illnesses. William Willimon's point needs to be heard.

The reality of low growth potential. Most churches that are not growing ought to feel concerned and attempt to do something about it. Some churches, however, such as those diagnosed as having ghost town disease, should be relieved of their guilt and encouraged to live the rest of their days in peace and comfort. This is why it is not advisable for a district superintendent or a state convention or a bishop to set a growth goal for the judicatory and then prorate uniform growth goals for each one of the churches in the judicatory, as many have tried to do. More times than not, this has produced frustration and failure to meet the goals.

Although it should be obvious, not every church leader has recognized the important fact that different churches have different growth potentials. The mix of contextual factors and institutional factors can vary enormously from church to church.

What is good growth for some churches might be poor growth for others.

The best procedure for setting growth goals for, let's say, a district, would be for the district superintendent to provide training for all the pastors in the district in the methodology of testing their churches for vital signs of health and for possible growth-inhibiting diseases. Using sound goal-setting principles, each pastor in conjunction with the local church lay leadership, then sets a realistic five-year goal for growth. The district superintendent receives and totals these individual church growth goals, adds them up, and this, along with goals

---

How should "success" be viewed in a church dying of ghost town disease? "Success will be the successful undertaking of whatever healing, guiding, sustaining, and reconciling acts are needed in a particular situation."

---

for planting new churches, becomes the goal for the district.

Denominational executives who have experimented with this procedure have frequently reported that the sum total is far greater than they would have dared to set themselves. The frustrations of the district office are thus greatly reduced because the responsibility for achieving the goals now rests with the local churches, each one of which owns its own goal.

Although we recognize that individual variations can be significant, it is still helpful to many to see in front of them a generalized scale of expected growth. The following scale has survived considerable scrutiny, and using the previously mentioned disclaimers, can be applied to local churches, judicatories and denominations:

> 25 percent per decade — poor growth
> 50 percent per decade — fair growth
> 100 percent per decade — good growth
> 200 percent per decade — excellent growth
> 300 percent per decade — outstanding growth
> 500 percent per decade — incredible growth

Many churches growing at only 25 percent per decade should be doing better, but for some it is satisfactory. Other churches that for some reason have been declining rather than growing can feel successful if they halt their decline and remain status quo for a couple of years. If the church is not growing well because it has a curable disease, the disease should be treated and the church should move forward. If the disease is terminal, no such unrealistic growth demands should be expected of the church.

How should "success" be viewed in a church dying of ghost town disease? "Success," says William Willimon, "will be the successful undertaking of whatever healing, guiding, sustaining, and reconciling acts are needed in a particular situation."[5] The more realistic both pastors and denominational executives are at this point, the better off the Body of Christ in general will be.

2. Honesty in Disclosure

The second felt need of churches having ghost town disease is, in my opinion, honesty in disclosure. I realize that medical doctors agonize about whether a human patient should be informed that he or she has a terminal illness, and if so, when. There is no easy answer to this question. In some situations it might be best that the patient does not know. In others, dying with dignity requires that the diagnosis be fully disclosed.

My feeling is that in the case of a church experiencing a terminal illness, the sooner the congregation understands and accepts its condition, the better. This is particularly true when a church has ethnikitis, but it also applies to ghost town disease. If the terminal condition is successfully dissociated from unfaithfulness to God or from spiritual deficiency or sin, the disclosure can usually be handled with grace.

Of course, it is important to make sure the diagnosis is accurate. It is possible, for example, to confuse ethnikitis with people-blindness, or ghost town disease with St. John's syndrome (see chapter 9). Diagnostic procedures for churches have improved a great deal in the past few years, and we can expect them to become more and more refined and thereby more accurate in the years to come. Meanwhile, caution is advised before pronouncing a church terminal.

Above all, churches experiencing terminal illnesses should

not be elevated continually by offering false hopes. Suggestions that if only the church could change pastors, add a Christian education facility, become more involved in community affairs, renovate the sanctuary, hire a minister of music or any number of other things do not help the situation. Many are willing to reduce church growth to a one-cause analysis: start expository preaching and your church will grow, develop a home cell system, begin early morning prayer meetings or whatever. If the church is going to die, prescribing the equivalent of vitamins or pep pills is not a good answer. Church leaders need to be warned that no quick fixes are available for their situations.

In our generation, a growing awareness of and interest in hospice care for terminal patients is occurring. I received a brochure from a hospice in Indiana that was founded on a well-stated principle: "Dying is a natural event, which, like birth, needs to be recognized and accepted without fear and with the assistance of family, friends, and the community." This could apply well to churches.

3. Sensitive Pastoral Care
The same brochure goes on to state that hospice care becomes appropriate "when comfort, rather than cure, is the primary focus of medical care."

Not every physician, or even every psychologist, knows how to handle dying patients well. Not every pastor has the gifts and the sensitivities required to handle a dying church well. For this reason, many pastors may seek reassignments or new callings as soon as they begin to suspect terminal illness is involved. This is an understandable and for some a necessary decision.

The people in a dying church, however, are still God's people. They are brothers and sisters in Christ. They cannot and ought not to be neglected. Contemporary American culture is often much too quick to relegate handicapped people to asylums and elderly people to rest homes. Our ecclesiastical society is likewise probably too quick to abandon the people in weak and diminishing churches. If we have room for specialists in Christian education, evangelism, visitation, music, worship and youth work, why not specialists in caring for congregations in churches experiencing ghost town disease?

I know many pastors who lack the gifts to set and implement bold growth goals, but they do love people. They are the ones who can handle hospice kind of care for dying churches. Perhaps denominational subsidies are needed here, at least to a point, because dying churches frequently have serious budgetary problems.

In any case, sensitive pastoral care is demanded for the people of God caught in America's dying churches. It is, after all, a biblical principle articulated in Galatians 6:2 to "Bear one another's burdens, and so fulfill the law of Christ."

A MINISTRY OF HOPE

It is not pleasant to write a whole chapter focused on a terminal illness. I am therefore most grateful to my friend Kent Hunter who is a positive thinker, and who has given me a quote that can end this chapter on an upbeat note: "The rural congregation of a shrinking church has an important ministry—a ministry of hope that goes beyond depression, love that surpasses despair, and life that transcends death itself. Ministry in a shrinking community is an opportunity to share the Good News with people who are surrounded with bad news."[6]

Notes

1. Edward W. Hassinger, John S. Holik and J. Kenneth Benson, *The Rural Church: Learning from Three Decades of Change* (Nashville: Abingdon Press, 1988), p. 67.
2. Kent R. Hunter, *The Lord's Harvest and the Rural Church* (Kansas City, Mo.: Beacon Hill Press, 1993), p. 49.
3. The story of Zion Church was taken from an article in *The Covenant Companion* (January 1, 1977): 18.
4. William H. Willimon, "Pastoral Care of Dying Churches," *The Christian Ministry* (March 1978): 7-30.
5. Ibid.
6. Hunter, *The Lord's Harvest*, p. 49.

Chapter 4

PEOPLE-BLINDNESS:
WHY DON'T
THEY LIKE US?

People-blindness, unlike ethnikitis or ghost town disease, is not terminal. It can be cured. Like every disease listed in this book about the pathology of churches, however, it can severely retard effective evangelism and stunt the growth of the church. It is helpful to recognize it, label it and understand its symptoms as thoroughly as possible.

Some churches seem to be in good health, fully motivated to grow and active in outreach and evangelism. Their evangelistic efforts, however, do not result in much church growth. Why?

In some cases the trouble might lie in the area of what we are calling people-blindness. Because it is a form of "blindness," however, the church may not have perceived the problem at all. A large number of churches I have studied are not only unaware of their people-blindness, but they are also in active denial that they could possibly get it.

E-1, E-2 AND E-3

To understand what is at the root of people-blindness, it is necessary first of all to become familiar with some terminology currently being used in the Church Growth Movement and among missiologists in general. Those who have been trained in church growth or who have been reading church growth literature will be familiar with the following designations: E-1, E-2 and E-3.

The symbol *E* stands for "evangelism," and the numbers stand for different cultural distances from the person or group initiating the evangelistic process. Thus, E-1, or "evangelism-one," signifies evangelism among people sharing the same culture as the evangelist or the evangelistic team. In contrast, both E-2 and E-3 represent the kind of evangelism necessary to win to Christ people of a different culture from that of the evangelist. E-1 is *monocultural* evangelism, and E-2 and E-3 are both *cross-cultural* evangelism.

The difference between E-2 and E-3 is a difference in degree only. Both are cross-cultural, but E-3 signifies a culture more radically different from that of the evangelist than E-2 would signify. All cultural distances are not equal. This can be illustrated easily by using cultures in various parts of the world as examples.

An Anglo-American from Cleveland, Ohio, for example, who would evangelize the French in a Paris suburb, would be doing E-2 evangelism. French culture is different from Anglo-American culture, but a common Latin and European influence provides many similarities. The same Anglo-American from Cleveland, going to evangelize Buddhists in Thailand, however, would find himself or herself in an E-3 situation. Thai culture is obviously much more distant from Anglo-American culture than is the French.

One does not have to leave America to find clear situations calling for E-2 and E-3 evangelism. An Anglo-American evangelizing Hispanic-Americans would be doing E-2, but evangelizing reservation Navajos would involve E-3. In many urban areas in the United States it would be possible to do E-1, E-2 and E-3 evangelism in the same neighborhood, and sometimes on the same block. The essential difference is not *geographical* (although geographical distance often plays a role), but *cultural*.

These distinctions are important in planning evangelistic strategies aimed at church growth. The method appropriate for reaching one people group can be different from methods used to reach other people groups. It also entails a clear range of difficulty, E-3 evangelism being the most difficult evangelistic challenge, E-2 the next most difficult and E-1 the easiest, in general terms. That is why in the United States and worldwide, most church growth across the board comes as a result of E-1 evangelism. E-2 and E-3, however, are absolutely essential if the gospel is to take root in new unchurched cultures.

THE HIGHEST PRIORITY

Incidentally, more than 70 percent of the world's unreached people can be reached only through cross-cultural evangelism. The A.D. 2000 and Beyond Movement estimates that approximately 1,700 significantly large people groups today know nothing about salvation through Jesus Christ. Thus, as far as world evangelization is concerned, E-2 and E-3 constitute the highest priority. Once strong biblical churches are established in another culture by E-2 or E-3, then E-1 evangelism will take over, the gospel will spread and churches will be multiplied

This is a familiar biblical pattern. To give just one illustration from the New Testament, two separate missions set out to evangelize the city of Antioch. The missionaries in both cases were Jews. In the target city of Antioch, which then had a population of 500,000, lived groups of both Jews and Gentiles. The first mission did E-1 evangelism and established churches among Jews only (see Acts 11:19).

Then about 10 years later, another mission was formed that I like to call the "C.C.M."—the Cyprus and Cyrene Mission. The evangelists of the C.C.M. specialized in E-2 or E-3 evangelism (whichever it might have been to them) in Antioch and began winning the *Gentiles* and establishing *Gentile* churches for the first time (see v. 20). Details of this instructive biblical example are found in my commentary on Acts, *Lighting the World* (Regal Books).

DEFINING PEOPLE-BLINDNESS

People-blindness is directly related to a lack of understanding of the significant differences between E-1 evangelism on the one hand, and E-2 and E-3 evangelism on the other. The terms themselves were first introduced by Ralph Winter, of the U.S. Center for World Mission, in his epochal address to the plenary session at the International Congress on World Evangelization, held in Lausanne, Switzerland, in 1974. His topic was, "The Highest Priority: Cross-Cultural Evangelism."[1]

In some cases, prejudice barriers that have been built up over generations can also effectively keep the message of the gospel from moving across cultural barriers from one people group to another.

We are now ready for a working definition of people-blindness:

People-blindness is the malady that prevents us from seeing the important cultural differences that exist between groups of people living in geographical proximity to one another—differences that tend to create barriers to the acceptance of our message.

Two problems that inhibit the evangelistic process become evident when people-blindness is present.

1. *Problems of transmitting the message.* The most obvious problem in cross-cultural evangelism is linguistic. When languages are mutually unintelligible, the message cannot get through. Even when the groups involved speak a mutually intelligible language, dialect differences and many nonverbal forms of communication tend to complicate the transmission of the message, as speakers of British English and American English will readily recognize. Some communications researchers will say that up to 90 percent of human communication is nonverbal.

As an example, living in New England are about 2 million French-speaking people known as "Francophones." Throughout the generations, New England churches have not been successful in evangelizing the Francophones, most of whom also speak English. Their approach has been the "open door policy" of inviting Francophones to come to their churches and worship with them. Although they sincerely love the French people and desire to win them to Christ, it has not happened to any significant degree.

The cause of this frustrating situation is people-blindness. Just because they understand English does not necessarily mean that Francophones will feel comfortable in Anglo-American churches. If any powerful evangelistic movement is ever to start among them, it will certainly be spearheaded by multiplying new churches in which the preachers, the choirs, the deacons and the Sunday School teachers are Francophones. If the French they speak is Quebec French as opposed to Parisian French, all the better.

In some cases, prejudice barriers that have been built up over generations can also effectively keep the message of the gospel from moving across cultural barriers from one people group to another. Granted, we must take every step possible to erase prejudice from our society, but until we are successful in that endeavor we must spread the gospel among those who are still prejudiced to one degree or another.

To use the technical language I introduced earlier, the root of evangelistic ineffectiveness attributed to people-blindness is *attempting to use E-1 evangelistic messages in a situation that calls for E-2 or E-3*. In other words, monocultural evangelistic strategies cannot work well in cross-cultural situations.

WINNING THE DEAF TO CHRIST

In the United States we have an estimated 14 million to 21 million deaf people, the difference being in the degree of hearing impairment we are using as a measurement. Among the deaf, only 8 percent are born again as compared to around 36 percent of Americans in general. Why is there such a dramatic disparity? Why are deaf people not being won to Christ as much as are hearing people? The answer lies in an easily diagnosable case of people-blindness.

Many churches sincerely want to minister to the deaf people in their community. They have attempted to do so by using three common approaches:

- Reserving a section for deaf people in the worship service, and signing the service for them.
- Doing the above, but also forming a distinct deaf fellowship group in a hearing church.
- Planting deaf churches in which the pastors, the lay leadership and the congregation are mostly deaf.

The first approach in the list has proved to be the least successful, and the last has been the most successful. Three denominations have developed enough people vision to implement aggressive programs for multiplying deaf churches: Assemblies of God, Lutheran Church Missouri Synod and Southern Baptists. The United Methodists and General Conference Mennonites, and perhaps others, are also moving in this direction.

The key to the success of these denominations has been to recognize that deaf culture is distinct enough from hearing culture to demand an E-2 evangelistic strategy rather than an E-1 strategy. The difference lies in realizing that to reach people in other cultures, a different *kind of church* is needed. Those of a different people group such as the deaf should not be expected to cross what they perceive to be formidable cultural barriers and join your church just because they are now converted to Christ.

2. Problems in "folding" new converts. In many cases, even if the message gets through and people become Christian believers, residual cultural differences make it virtually impossible to fold that new convert in any meaningful way into the fellowship of the church to which the evangelist belongs. Some critics find biblical passages they interpret as saying this ought not to be. Some try to wish it away. I personally join them in the desire that it were not true. Sociologically, what I have stated is a simple fact of life and, as we shall see, if we do not accept it as a fact and plan accordingly it may very well shut the door on effective evangelism.

Clearly discernible elements of American social history have made it difficult for many Americans to admit that important differences among subgroupings of American citizens exist. Although significant changes have come in our generation, through most of American history the American dream encouraged us to believe that our nation is a "melting pot," and that all Americans are, or eventually will be, one culture indivisible.

Because all Americans are presumed to have equal rights under the laws of our land, it seems to be a fair conclusion that we all should be one. In that case, all Americans could be reached for Christ by the same methods. If that were so, I could expect that anyone, regardless of race, class, national origin or regional identity would feel comfortable in joining my church if that person becomes a Christian. If my church is good enough for me and my family, it should be good enough for anyone else.

Such conclusions, still common today despite our growing national awareness of multiculturalism, are typical of those afflicted with people-blindness. It is this mind-set that, more frequently than we would wish, retards the spread of the gospel and stunts the growth of many churches.

This viewpoint is appealing because it stresses that since Christ has broken down the middle wall of partition (see Eph. 2:14), and that in Christ there is no Greek or Jew or barbarian or Scythian or slave or free (see Col. 3:11), all people, despite cultural or lifestyle or linguistic differences should expect to fit together harmoniously in the same local congregation.

In my opinion, however, those who arrive at such conclusions are reading the Bible with people-blindness. They fail to see the validity of the decisive methods that led to the great E-2 and E-3 evangelistic thrusts—first from Hebrew Jews to Hellenistic Jews, then from Jews in general to Samaritans, then from Jews to Gentiles. In each case, new culturally relevant churches were formed. Conglomerate congregations, as we learn from Acts 6:1-7 where the Hebrew segment of the church in Jerusalem divided from the Hellenistic segment, were generally not feasible.

The so-called Judaizers in the New Testament times were afflicted with people-blindness and they aggressively opposed the formation of Gentile churches. They, instead, wanted all the new Gentile believers to behave like Jews. Paul's Epistles, however, especially Galatians, and the Jerusalem Council (see Acts 15), affirmed the validity of culturally distinct churches for culturally distinct peoples. The apostle Paul and the Jerusalem Council did not suffer from people-blindness as the Judaizers did.

The Judaizers represented the most extreme form of the disease, that of cultural chauvinism. They believed that their Jewish culture was *superior to*, not just *different from*, that of the Gentiles. Of course, they tried to give good theological reasons for why that was true, but they failed. There are no good theological reasons for suggesting that the way to eliminate group differences is for others to become "just like us."

I realize that many who read this will have serious questions in their minds about the validity of my biblical interpretation. For this reason I studied and taught Acts for 15 years and put my findings into a three-volume commentary, which traces this theme (as well as others) through the book of Acts verse by verse. In it, those who are interested will find more material about the cross-cultural dimensions of the spread of the gospel than in other commentaries.[2]

This kind of assimilationist philosophy, characteristic of the Judaizers in New Testament times, had been common among Anglo-Americans up to the civil rights movements of the 1960s. Since then, however, the strong voices of minority groups have made us realize that the melting-pot theory may, all along, have constituted a kind of cultural chauvinism on the part of Anglo-Americans.

The trend today is to recognize that not only is black beautiful, but that all the other cultural minority groups in America are also beautiful. It is helping us to recover from our innate American tendencies toward people-blindness. It also may reduce our inclination to justify the American dream of the "melting pot" through quoting biblical proof texts.

Research into the way churches ordinarily grow has shown conclusively that evangelistic efforts are relatively ineffective when based on the notion that all kinds of people should be encouraged to join the same local congregation. Those who attempt to conduct such evangelism suffer from people-blindness. They are making a fundamental sociological error, almost equivalent to attempting to defy the law of gravity.

SOCIOLOGICAL TISSUE REJECTION

People-blindness usually carries with it the inability to understand an important human phenomenon I like to describe as "sociological tissue rejection." Medical science has discovered that blood transfusions and organ transplants from one body to another will be successful only to the degree that the types of blood or other tissue of the two persons involved match. If there is incompatibility between the organs, rejection will occur.

For reasons we do not fully understand, but we nevertheless must accept, God so made the human body that it prefers death to accepting foreign tissue, when that tissue is not a satisfactory match. This medical law of nature applies equally to believers and unbelievers. Conversion to Christianity does not allow a person who has type A blood to receive a transfusion of type B blood and survive.

Although we accept the unfortunate reality of physical tissue rejection, we seem to have a much more difficult time accepting a similar phenomenon when applied to the social aspect of human life. It is a social fact, however, that some groups of people prefer the death or dissolution of their group to the alternative of accepting people into their group whom they perceive, for whatever reasons, as being incompatible. Something deeply inherent in human social psychology, whether in believers or unbelievers, tends to force them, consciously or unconsciously, to reject the foreign tissue.

Some Christian leaders spend a great deal of time trying to change this phenomenon. They might as well spend their time trying to make the Mississippi River flow north. There are, of course, some exceptions to this just as there are some stretches of the Mississippi where the water actually does flow north. But the exceptions do not change the rule. Churches around the world and throughout history have grown basically among one kind of people at a time, and they show every indication that they will continue growing that way until the Lord returns.

Overcoming people-blindness is not simple. Blood types and Rh factors are easier to acknowledge than are social types and their interrelationships. Whereas, for example, distinctions between Anglo-Americans and African-Americans and Hispanic-Americans and Asian-Americans are obvious to anyone who has physical sight, that is only the beginning. The many subdivisions within each group are extremely important for church growth, but they are much more complex. The ability to discern and respect such divisions I call "people-vision," just the opposite of people-blindness.

Among Hispanic-Americans, for example, the differences between Cuban-Americans, Spanish-Americans, Puerto Ricans and Mexican-Americans is important. Further, there are extremely important differences among Mexican-Americans themselves. Mexican-Americans in southern Texas are different from Mexican-Americans in northern New Mexico, and both groups are different from Chicanos in California's San Joaquin Valley. Some Mexican-Americans in Los Angeles, for example, speak mostly English in their homes, live in integrated neighborhoods and have well-paying white-collar jobs. Other Mexican-Americans live in East Los Angeles *barrios*—they are undocumented, their youth belong to gangs and their family incomes are often at or below the poverty level. Although both groups could be described as "Los Angeles Mexican-Americans," they are vastly different from one another and in all probability would not successfully be folded into the same congregations, even if they become committed Christians.

A study has shown that of the hundreds of Hispanic-American churches in the Los Angeles area, only 12 percent mix different kinds of Hispanics to any significant degree. Most churches are well known in their communities as either Mexican, Mexican-American, Cuban, Puerto Rican, Salvadoran, South American or whatever.

FREEDOM IN ROLLING HILLS

A subtle group difference, this time among Anglo-Americans, was emphasized to me when I visited Rolling Hills Covenant Church. Rolling Hills is located south of Los Angeles on what is called The Peninsula. Housing is expensive, it is crisscrossed with bridle paths, and the residents are yacht and country club types. Rolling Hills Church is winning these people in large numbers, and it is growing fast. It may have the highest number of surgeons per capita of any church in the Los Angeles area.

During my visit I had a long conversation with a surgeon's wife. She was vivacious, well-groomed, cultured and an enthusiastic, active Christian. She believed that her spiritual gifts were being used in Rolling Hills Covenant Church and her Christian life was a joy. However, it had not always been that way.

She and her husband had previously attended a small Baptist church in which the members were also good Christians, evangelistically minded, friendly and open to new people. But they were people of a lower socioeconomic level, and try as they would, the women of that church simply did not know how to relate to this surgeon's wife. She constantly felt frustrated. She tried to start Bible study classes, but they never seemed to get off the ground. She began to wonder if there might be something wrong with her spiritual life.

When she and her husband transferred to Rolling Hills

Social differences between groups of people must be kept in mind when churches plan evangelistic programs. They are crucial for both expansion growth (receiving new members into the present congregation), and for extension growth (starting new churches).

Covenant, it was a different story. Without forcing anything, she could now relate to the people on a peer level. She started new Bible studies and they were very popular. For the first time, she felt she was being fulfilled in her Christian ministry and was the woman God wanted her to be.

The difference was not in the orthodoxy of the church or the friendliness of the people or the presence of the Holy Spirit or in her own personal walk before the Lord. The difference was basically sociocultural. Sociological tissue rejection had been active, although it was undetected and would have been denied if someone had raised the question. Only those who have people-vision could see, understand and creatively cope with the difference.

Such social differences between groups of people must be

kept in mind when churches plan evangelistic programs. They are crucial for both expansion growth (receiving new members into the present congregation), and for extension growth (starting new churches). If your evangelistic program has as its goal folding the new converts into your present congregation, take the time beforehand to understand the "group type" of your own church and the "group types" in your community. Then direct your initial efforts toward those neighborhoods and people who best match. This is the most effective way to achieve E-1 evangelism.

DEATH IN THE NURSERY

A case of E-2 evangelism having results that were unanticipated because of people-blindness occurred in two New Jersey cities, Franklin and Neptune. The Department of Church Extension of the Bible Fellowship Church had started new Bible Fellowship churches in both of these towns. Each one of the churches was around four years old when it died.

The Bible Fellowship Church is a small denomination of about 50 churches in Eastern Pennsylvania and New Jersey. The denomination is evangelistically oriented and has been growing. Like many other denominations, throughout its history it has established and maintained certain membership requirements that it believes are in accordance with the Scriptures. These concern some lifestyle rules that are not necessarily agreed upon by all Christians, even by evangelical Christians who mutually accept the Bible as their ultimate authority for faith and practice.

I should mention that such membership requirements usually are a sign of strength, not weakness, in a church. Dean Kelley's classic book *Why Conservative Churches Are Growing* has provided coherent sociological explanation for why this would be true. In recounting this case, I am not suggesting that the Bible Fellowship Church, or any other denomination, should water down its membership requirements. I am simply showing how using E-1 methods for E-2 evangelism can kill churches.

As long as the new groups were seen as "missions," they experienced few problems. When they began to mature and then applied for full membership in the denomination, on a par with the existing churches, however, some differences became evident.

The families who had been won into the new churches in Franklin and Neptune happened to have a different cultural orientation from that of the traditional Bible Fellowship members. As frequently happens in cross-cultural situations, they studied the same Bible, but came to different conclusions about how its teachings should be applied to contemporary life. Some of the particular areas that were called into question concerned divorce, tobacco and alcohol. The issues were reminiscent of New Testament times when eating meat offered to idols was discussed, and now, as then, there were at least two points of view.

After much negotiation and discussion, the issue came to a head. The Bible Fellowship Church decided it would maintain its strict requirements and not admit the new churches unless they conformed. The result was that both of the young churches became disheartened and died a premature death. In retrospect, one might expect that the new churches would have been encouraged to continue, either as independent organizations, or as part of some denomination holding compatible views. To suggest either of these options, however, would have required an extraordinarily high degree of people-vision. Under the circumstances, the Bible Fellowship Church probably made the right decision, but it cannot expect to do much effective E-2 evangelism adhering to such a policy.[3]

IS THIS DISCRIMINATION?

Understanding the difference between E-1 evangelism and E-2 or E-3 evangelism is not in any way to be confused with racism or discrimination. No church should be closed to receiving members from other racial or social groups who desire to unite with the church. Such a position has no proper place in the kingdom of God. Christians, because they have the love of the Holy Spirit in their hearts, can and do make the necessary adjustments to mix people from different groups, for the mutual enrichment of all concerned. Churches that major in doing this and build high-priority programs around it, however, most often find themselves losing evangelistic power and becoming increasingly irrelevant to the *unbelievers* among all the groups concerned.

It is much more effective to gather people from a certain social group into a congregation composed basically of other people from that particular group. Once this is done, the resulting congregations should relate to one another with a spirit of love and interdependence, each with respect for the other's lifestyle and cultural integrity. The larger a local church is, the more congregational subgroupings from diverse cultures can occur within the total membership group. More often than not, however, separate churches will have a more powerful evangelistic influence on the community.

A THIN, BUT IMPORTANT, LINE

As a final illustration, Charles Mylander, at the time one of the pastors of Rose Drive Friends Church in Orange County, California, conducted a study of a phenomenon he discovered operating between his church and the Yorba Linda Friends Church, only two miles away.[4] Here were two churches of the same denomination, both essentially white Anglo-American congregations. The members lived generally in the same areas, both churches had lovely facilities and both were growing well.

The pastors of both churches, however, gradually became aware that some people would show up at one church for a month or so and then disappear, only to be found later as full, active members of the other church. Mylander, who has good people-vision, went to work to discover why this might be happening.

Mylander found that although by most external criteria the churches seemed virtually identical, they really were two distinct groups of people. The differences were extremely subtle. They resulted from slight variations in educational levels, occupational roles and housing choices. These factors apparently were strong enough so that the people directly involved knew that for some reason they felt uncomfortable in one church, but at home in the other. Without fully realizing it, they were looking for a church attended by "their kind of people."

In this case, the fact that two Friends churches instead of just one were located in that part of Orange County increased the evangelistic potential of each of them. The members of both churches maintain good relationships, engage in some joint programs and love one another in the Lord. Their distinctive personalities or "group types" are regarded by them as a strength, not a weakness.

THE CURE FOR PEOPLE-BLINDNESS

The remedy for people-blindness is twofold: first theological, and then anthropological.

Theologically, moving from people-blindness to people-vision will require some deprogramming in many cases. The guilt feelings present in American social psychology as a result of centuries of racism and discrimination have been reflected in theologies. Some Christian theologians and ethicists have advocated an assimilationist stance toward minority groups in America, and have attempted to justify the melting pot in theological terms. Many current American pastors were trained in seminaries that advocated assimilation. It will take some theological rethinking to accept a position of respecting different cultural groups for what they are, and of affirming their desire, if and when it is present, to maintain their own cultural identity and integrity. When this happens, the value of churches as authentic reflections of "their" culture, and not only of "ours," will be more and more appreciated.

Anthropologically, sensitivity to the significant components of culture and the way these can be recognized needs to be developed. Furthermore, anthropological insights help to reduce cultural chauvinism and allow people to recognize that although "our" culture might be *different* from "theirs," we need not assume that it is *better* than theirs. Whenever this happens, increased tolerance will help build respect for churches that might differ from ours regarding the specific application and interpretation of biblical principles.

The net result of dispelling people-blindness will be an increased effectiveness in evangelistic efforts, as well as an increased harmony, understanding and mutual interdependence among Christians of different races and social classes.

Notes

1. Ralph D. Winter, "The Highest Priority: Cross-Cultural Evangelism," J. D. Douglas, ed., *Let the Earth Hear His Voice* (Minneapolis: World Wide Publishers, 1975), pp. 213-25.
2. The three volumes of Acts by C. Peter Wagner are *Spreading the Fire, Lighting the World and Blazing the Way*, all published by Regal Books.
3. The data for this example are taken from *Tie Lines* 6, nos. 1, 3 (1976), a newsletter published by the Department of Church Extension of the Bible Fellowship Church.
4. Charles E. Mylander, "Suburban Friends Growth" (Pasadena: Fuller Theological Seminary, unpublished doctoral dissertation, 1975), p. 10.

Chapter 5

HYPER-COOPERATIVISM: WHEN UNITY HINDERS EVANGELISM

We live in an age when church cooperation, both formal and informal, is considered a high value. The World Council of Churches is a pioneer in international church unity. The National Association of Evangelicals gains strength in America each year. Separatism, fashionable during the 1930s and 1940s, seems to have little appeal to the general evangelical public anymore. Staunch denominational loyalty among church members is at a low ebb; many people nowadays look for more than traditional denominational distinctives in a local church they are considering joining.

Cooperation being the "in" thing these days, the danger of what we are calling hyper-cooperativism increases. I need to say here that this chapter is in no way intended to suggest that interchurch cooperation is a bad thing in itself nor is it a church disease. It is not in any way an antiecumenical polemic. I believe we need more Christian unity manifested in more tangible ways, not less.

Jesus' prayer "that they also may be one...that the world may believe" (John 17:21) is a directional word for us today. Those familiar with my writings about spiritual warfare will know I am convinced that the wider the agreement we have among Christians, the greater will be our spiritual power as a church. Having said that, I will nevertheless argue in this chapter that cooperation among churches is more useful for accomplishing certain goals than it is for others.

Interchurch cooperation can be useful for social action projects, for providing relief to victims of earthquakes or famines, for sponsoring theological seminaries, for promoting cordial relationships between ministers and for programs of joint enrichment among churches of different cultures. It can also be useful for militant spiritual warfare over a city, for taking public positions on certain political issues such as abortion or taxation of church properties, or even for projects involving E-2 or E-3 evangelism at home and abroad. If our goal at the moment is evangelism that will result in church growth on the *local* level, however, the cooperative programs that have been tried to date have not proven effective.

Church cooperation, as I have said, is a good thing. *Hypercooperativism* occurs, however, when an attempt is made to use cooperation for unwise purposes. It is frequently not just neutral, but in certain circumstances it can become counterproductive.

A FALSE PREMISE

For at least three decades, evangelicals, who have typically professed to be committed to effective evangelism and church growth, have been told that one way to evangelize more effectively is to cooperate interdenominationally on a local or regional level. Citywide evangelistic efforts have become popular and have constituted a prominent method of doing evangelization in America since the early '50s, and even before.

Some of the parachurch evangelistic agencies that have materialized have solicited resources both from the churches of a given city and from their church members to conduct a program of citywide evangelism. Their premise, whether explicit or implied, has been that through supporting the city-wide cooperative evangelistic effort, more unbelievers will be won to Christ and folded into the participating churches than without it. Some evangelists will not accept an invitation to come to a city unless a certain degree of interchurch support for the crusade is secured beforehand. The underlying assumption is that the more cooperation, the more fruit will be born by the evangelistic project.

This premise has shown little or no evidence that it is valid. Research done to date about citywide evangelism seems to indicate that just the opposite may frequently be true—the more churches cooperate interdenominationally in evangelistic projects, the less effectively they evangelize.

Of the several reasons hyper-cooperativism frequently reduces evangelistic effectiveness, perhaps the most important is that cooperative efforts tend to dilute the centrality of the local church. Citywide evangelistic efforts involving the churches of just one denomination may have more potential than interdenominational efforts, but the strongest of all is local church evangelism.

In the typical citywide effort, the meetings are held in a neutral place, such as a stadium or a civic auditorium, and consequently in the minds of the unbelievers who attend, there is no natural or necessary connection between making a decision for Christ and commitment to a local church. Unless the local church remains central, the kind of evangelism that produces fruit that remains and results in church growth will be minimal.

POSITIVE EFFECTS OF
COOPERATIVE EVANGELISM

Evaluation of the results of any evangelistic program will, naturally, depend on the goals set for it. The assumption in this book, as in all church growth writings, is that evangelism should result in church growth. The premise is that a thorough conversion will involve a dual commitment: (1) commitment to Jesus Christ and (2) commitment to the Body of Christ. An important difference must be kept in mind between evangelism that results in *decisions* for Christ and evangelism that results in *disciples* of Christ.

Having said this, however, it must also be added that many

citywide evangelistic efforts have brought positive results that cannot be measured directly in church growth. Some of them are as follows:

E-0 Evangelism

In the previous chapter, we described E-1, E-2 and E-3 evangelism. E-0 evangelism is the other category in the series. It signifies winning to Christ a person who is already a church member, but who has never made a personal commitment to Christ. Theoretically, all church members should have made a commitment to Christ, but we all know that many have not. The percentage will vary from church to church, but virtually every church has some members who are not yet saved or committed or born again or converted or whatever terminology may be appropriate to a certain tradition.

Recent surveys show that although 56 percent of American adults are active church members, only 36 percent are born-again Christians. That leaves 20 percent who probably need E-0 evangelism. We are probably talking about 50 million people!

When E-0 evangelism occurs, the church, of course, does not grow visibly, because the individuals are already members. But it becomes a better church. It grows in quality; and that is certainly a commendable thing.

A Rite of Passage

Anthropologists tell us that most societies have developed certain prescribed ceremonies that give visible public sanction to the milestone events in the life cycle of individuals. Big evangelistic crusades provide occasions for such so-called "rites of passage," both for the children of believers who feel a need to express their faith publicly, and for others who may have already decided to become Christians and who are looking for an appropriate opportunity to finalize their decisions. In all probability, both of these kinds of people would have eventually made professions of faith with or without the crusade, but the citywide evangelistic crusade is as good an opportunity as any to do it.

Public Exposure to the Gospel

Citywide crusades tend to bring Jesus Christ to a high level of public attention. Television and radio spots, billboards, bumper stickers, large meetings reported in the newspapers, all help to draw public attention to the message. How much this actually aids in the total process of evangelization may vary according to the situation. Its effectiveness also depends on the previous level of awareness of the general public. In most cases, it can be listed as another positive benefit.

Privatized Christians

As Thomas Luckmann and other sociologists of religion have pointed out, the phenomenon of "privatized religion" has been on the increase in America. Although this includes religious expressions other than Christianity, undoubtedly, an increasing number of Americans may have been reconciled to God through Jesus Christ, but they do not belong to a church, nor do they have any immediate intention of joining one. Many undoubtedly are TV Christians. In their pajamas and slippers, they may watch Robert Schuller or Jerry Falwell or James Kennedy or others, while sipping coffee and munching a Danish pastry. They send contributions to these programs, and consider them their surrogate churches.

Undoubtedly, many such TV Christians are truly committed to Jesus Christ. They grow in their faith Sunday by Sunday. They read the Bible and pray regularly. The Church Growth Movement, however, considers this an incomplete commitment. As I have said, we teach that a full commitment to Jesus Christ involves a simultaneous commitment to His Body, the Church. The Bible indicates that authentic Christians are to relate to each other in the Body of Christ (see 1 Cor. 12), using their spiritual gifts to minister to one another.

Some, of course, are privatized Christians by necessity. They are aged or disabled and could not leave home and attend church if they wanted to. Others are TV Christians by choice. Although I must admit that it is better to be a privatized Christian than no Christian at all, I do not believe this should be encouraged as a substitute for responsible church membership. Nevertheless, it must be affirmed that Christians who may not join churches are often a fruit of citywide evangelistic efforts.

FALLING SHORT OF EXPECTATIONS

E-0 evangelism, evangelistic rites of passage, increased public exposure to the gospel message, and privatized Christians are all positive results of cooperative evangelism. But none of them fully meets the expectations of the average pastor who leads the church into special large-scale evangelism programs. Deep

---

Going, preaching, baptizing, teaching and whatever else is necessary to make disciples—these are all important, but the final goal is to <u>make disciples</u>.

---

down in their hearts, local church pastors want those programs to help their churches grow through reaching unchurched men and women with the message of Christ and folding them into fellowship in their congregations. To the degree that this doesn't happen, they predictably feel let down.

Biblically, the goal of the Great Commission is to make disciples. Making disciples is the only imperative verb in the Commission as found in Matthew:

> "Go therefore and make disciples of all the nations, baptizing them in the name of the Father and of the Son and of the Holy Spirit, teaching them to observe all things that I have commanded you" (Matt. 28:19,20).

Going, preaching, baptizing, teaching and whatever else is necessary to make disciples—these are all important, but the final goal is to *make disciples*. In a rare exception or two, such as Joseph of Arimathea, biblical disciples were what we would today call church members. They are described as continuing "steadfastly in the apostles' doctrine and fellowship, and in breaking of bread, and in prayers" (Acts 2:42). When authentic disciples are made, churches add them to their numbers and grow.

Evangelistic associations that report their final results in terms of attendance at crusades, decisions recorded, Bible studies joined or anything less than responsible church membership, are fulfilling the Great Commission only partially. The very nature of most cooperative evangelism, as we have seen, hinders making church membership the bottom line against which to measure and report their success or failure.

THE FOLLOW-UP GAP

I began to understand some of the reasons for what I like to call the "follow-up gap" when I studied the vast Evangelism in Depth program conducted in Latin America some years ago. The follow-up gap, in my definition, is the difference between the number of persons who make recorded first-time decisions for Christ during an evangelistic effort and those among them who eventually become responsible church members.

Evangelism in Depth was the largest-scale attempt at cooperative evangelism in the history of Latin American Protestantism. It involved, for an entire year, virtually all of the Protestant churches in a given nation. Behind it were some of the best evangelical minds, and the program was originally designed specifically to correct the follow-up gap discovered in crusade evangelism. Despite all the prayer and money and personnel invested in a large number of Latin American nations, however, the follow-up gap persisted after the dust of the excitement had settled.

Hyper-cooperativism was by no means the only element contributing to the lackluster showing of Evangelism in Depth. It was, however, one of the more significant factors. It tended to reduce the message to the least common denominator. In one country, for example, the so-called *Wordless Book* was banned from the children's program because the committee chairperson disliked the red page, which was designed to teach children about the blood of Christ. The program attempted to keep the focus sufficiently on the local church, but the total effect on church growth was disappointing.

Significantly, toward the end of the decade when disillusionment with Evangelism in Depth was surfacing, some denominations were severely criticized for refusing to enter the nationwide program when it came to their countries. Their feeling that Evangelism in Depth would tend to retard their already vigorous growth patterns was not considered legitimate. Some were accused of being divisive because they chose not to cooperate. Those denominations for the most part, however, weathered the accusations and kept growing because they believed they could evangelize better by doing their own thing in their own way. The end result was that they were probably right.

KEY 73 AND HERE'S LIFE

The attempt to apply the methods of Evangelism in Depth to the United States came in what was called the Key 73 program. In 1973, the most massive coordinated evangelistic effort that America had yet known was conducted. Expectations were high, but the results were disappointing to the majority of cooperating churches, largely due, once again, to hyper-cooperativism. In this case, an inordinate amount of energy was demanded of church leaders across the board to accomplish the immense task of building bonds of interdenominational communication and cooperation. If ecumenism and cooperation had been the stated goals, Key 73 would have been a singular success. The *Christianity Today* editorial that originally sparked the entire movement used as its title: "Somehow, Let's Get Together." Unintentionally, and often quite subtly, cooperation might have been a higher priority in the minds of some than evangelism.

Evangelism, according to some analysts, entered the picture as only a means toward the real end, which was cooperation. Nevertheless, the overall goal was communicated to the average pastor in the pulpit as being evangelism, and most of them hoped against hope that Key 73 would be the program that would help their churches grow. When it didn't work out that way, they became disillusioned. Memories have faded since 1973, but widespread desire for national cooperation in evangelism has not reached that level since then. The positive recollections of Key 73 that remain in the minds of those who participated relate mostly to new friendships and improved Christian relationships, but not to accelerated church growth.

A few years later, Campus Crusade for Christ launched a

large national effort called "Here's Life, America." Large numbers of churches in virtually every city in the United States joined in the effort to evangelize the nation. Once again, evidence surfaced that as the program was being implemented city by city, cooperation had become a higher functional priority than had evangelism.

As an example, the *Here's Life America Southern California Communiqué* reported a meeting of 42 pastors from divergent denominational backgrounds. It reported how they discovered their mutual devotion to Jesus and how together they were uniting in a new way of corporate church life. The article quoted the leaders as saying that "this meeting alone was enough to make the entire Here's Life effort worthwhile." Although I would not want to push it too far, nevertheless, in the minds of those who originally designed the effort, the only thing that could possibly have made it worthwhile was not warm fellowship among believers, but saving lost souls! Many leaders had lost sight of this goal.

The evangelistic results of Here's Life were rather disappointing. Of those who made first-time decisions for Christ, only approximately 3 percent became church members.[1] Even allowing for those persons who may have received E-0 evangelism and those who became privatized Christians, there appears to be a disproportionately large follow-up gap.

CHALLENGES OF THE CHAPLAINCY

One of the most institutionalized examples of hyper-cooperativism in the United States is the military chaplaincy. I have spoken with many chaplains who are evangelistic in outlook and who would like their chapels to be effective centers for evangelism. Most of them are frustrated. Chapel growth on a military base is difficult to attain. The major reason for this might be a congenital case of hyper-cooperativism.

Protestant military chapels, according to regulations, have to be nondenominational. This is a distinct disadvantage. Under these rules, it is difficult for a chapel to develop a distinct philosophy of ministry geared specifically to the needs of a given target group. To suppose military personnel constitute a homogeneous unit that could be naturally drawn together in one congregation is naive. The total ministry on a given base might be strengthened if the chaplains were encouraged to be more distinctive in their chapels, but this does not seem to be a possibility in the near future. Thus, success for most chaplains will have to be gauged in some terms other than chapel growth, given the present conditions, which to all intents and purposes dictate hyper-cooperativism.

SCHALLER ON COOPERATION

One of America's outstanding church diagnosticians, Lyle E. Schaller, has come to similar conclusions concerning hyper-cooperativism and church growth. He says, "While this runs completely counter to the hopes and expectations of the advocates of church unity and intercongregational cooperation, the evidence is increasingly persuasive. Church growth and cooperative ministries are not compatible!"[2]

Schaller's five reasons concerning hyper-cooperativism and lack of church growth bear examination and commentary as a summary to this chapter. To the degree they are understood, hyper-cooperativism can be avoided.

1. *"A cooperative ministry may blur the distinctive identity of each participating congregation."*[3] This was seen in the case of the military chaplaincy. Churches that have a well-understood philosophy of ministry have growth advantages over churches that continually have to ask themselves, "Why are we here, anyway? What is our specific contribution to the kingdom of God?" Fuzzy answers to these questions will lessen growth potential.

2. *"People unite with a specific worshipping congregation, not with a cooperative ministry."*[4] There are some exceptions to this, as Schaller admits, but it is generally true. This is a chief reason that it is not conducive to eventual church membership if the person's decision for Christ is made in a neutral public place such as a stadium, particularly in the midst of a week or two of high-energy meetings. The new Christian may attend several crusade rallies that focus on their spotlights and crowds and 300-voice choirs and celebrities. It is a tough act for any local church to follow, and when reality sets in, disappointment often sets in.

3. *"People with a strong interest in evangelism and church growth rarely are interested in interchurch cooperation and vice versa."*[5] The exception to this is the parachurch evangelistic

associations, which have strong interests in evangelism and by their very natures depend on interchurch cooperation for exercising their ministries. That is certainly true of many dynamic, growing local churches. Participating in cooperative evangelism is frequently determined by a different kind of motivation. These churches may not think they need the city-wide effort for church growth and vitality, but at the same time they are aware of the effort's high visibility in the community and thereby understand that if they choose not to participate, their decisions would likely be interpreted as unsupportive of Christian unity. This is not the public image they desire, so they frequently go along with the movement, although somewhat reluctantly.

4. *"Many cooperative ministries come into existence as the result of pressures of dwindling resources."*[6] Church mergers, in particular, are often a clear sign of approaching decline, if not death. On the other hand, church splits, whether unintentional or planned, are often signs of vitality and growth. Cell division, not cell fusion, produces healthy, growing bodies.

5. *"Interchurch cooperation does use the time and energy of ministers and laity in creating and maintaining a new institution, and thus that time is not available for membership outreach."*[7] The broader the cooperation, the more complex the social relationships necessary to hold it together. Add to this the seemingly incompatible doctrines and policies, and the result is an association that is extremely demanding of available energy.

In a more recent work, Lyle Schaller applies these principles directly to the reasons certain churches grow and others do not. He says, "It is only a minor exaggeration to suggest that [the compulsion for promoting interchurch cooperation] is one of the most influential differences between large and numerically growing congregations and most small churches. The former assume that competition is the norm. The latter believe that cooperation should be the norm. That difference in perspective is one more reason why large congregations are large and small churches are small!"[8]

IS THERE ANY HOPE?

Because both evangelism that helps churches grow and interchurch cooperation are commendable activities, it seems reasonable to assume that there must be some way to join the two. Putting past disappointments to one side, it does appear now that some models for programs of cooperative evangelism, that in fact do result in measurable church growth, are emerging on the horizon.

Edgardo Silvoso, an Argentine evangelist, is one of the foremost leaders in developing strategies for evangelizing cities

When churches cooperating with citywide crusades are not in a healthy growth pattern themselves, the big meetings or the media blitz will not usually stimulate real growth. When the church is already growing,...the event can then help the churches to grow.

that combine the two. Silvoso's pilot project, called the "Rosario Plan," was designed and executed in Rosario, Argentina, in 1975 and 1976. More than half of the Protestant churches in the city joined the movement, so it was a good example of interchurch cooperation. The difference was that as early as 15 months before the public evangelistic event—which featured Silvoso's brother-in-law, Luis Palau—teams of church growth experts, including Vergil Gerber, Juan Carlos Miranda, Edward Murphy and Silvoso, worked with the cooperating churches. They helped each church develop plans and goals for growth in its own congregation, as well as in new churches they would plant.

Approximately 40 churches decided to cooperate. By the time Palau arrived, 45 *new* churches had been established. A strong growth process had been initiated, and new converts were already being made at rates not seen in Rosario for years. The evangelistic event then was introduced into the growth process at the most appropriate time. The evangelist was coming, not to *begin* the harvest, but rather to *accelerate* a harvest already begun. The barns were by then ready for the increased harvest, so to speak.

In the traditional models of citywide cooperative evangelism, between 3 percent and 16 percent of those who make first-time decisions for Christ become responsible members of the local churches. In Rosario, however, of the decisions registered during Palau's meetings, an amazing 57 percent were incorporated as members of churches. The follow-up gap had been considerably reduced.

THE PROCESS AND THE EVENT

As I see it, the secret of the success of the Rosario Plan, compared to the more traditional models of communitywide efforts in other cities, is skillfully coordinating the evangelistic event by using a growth process in the cooperating churches. When churches cooperating with citywide crusades are not in a healthy growth pattern themselves, the big meetings or the media blitz will not usually stimulate real growth. When the church is already growing, however, and when it is in the habit of folding in new converts *before* the start of the large, public evangelistic event, the event can then help the churches to grow. The following are two examples:

1. In 1969 when Billy Graham conducted his crusade in Anaheim, California, many Orange County churches reported a pleasant, stimulating experience, but little resultant growth. On the other hand, The Crystal Cathedral, which already had been growing at a 10-year rate of more than 500 percent, received hundreds of new members. The church had been tuned up for the crusade by previous growth momentum. It knew well how to take care of new converts. It was ready for the harvest.

2. The national follow-up rate for Here's Life America was 3 percent. Lake Avenue Congregational Church in Pasadena, California, however, which had previously developed a sophisticated pattern of folding new converts by Pastor Kent Tucker, folded 30 of 74 decisions, a rate of 42 percent. The evangelistic event helped both The Crystal Cathedral and Lake Avenue

because it fit properly into an already established
growth pattern.

My view is that a long-range component of church growth
planning and consultation should be provided as part and
parcel of a great high-visibility evangelistic event sponsored
by some interdenominational association. This should start as
much as one or two years before the event. The timing of the
event itself needs to remain flexible until all cooperating
churches (or a predetermined percentage of them) have corrected the problems causing their nongrowth or slow growth
and are reasonably sure that by the time of the event they will
be growing and absorbing new converts. When the cooperating churches are growing at an estimable rate, bring on the
evangelist or the media blitz or whatever method may be
appropriate. The follow-up gap will narrow dramatically
because the barns will be ready for the harvest.

This kind of thing can be done well through interchurch
cooperation. Because the primary growth goals are not
focused on the stadium, but on the local church, the local
churches remain central to the program. Many local churches
together can combine their resources to pay for areawide
media, the professional evangelist and the church growth consultation services, which most local churches by themselves
might not be able to afford.

THAT NONE SHOULD PERISH

Edgardo Silvoso contracted a life-threatening disease soon
after the Rosario Plan had ended and he was forced to curtail
his ministry for the better part of a decade. The Lord healed
him miraculously, though, and he is once again strategizing
citywide evangelism, this time using the added dimensions of
power healing, prayer and spiritual warfare. Silvoso's book
That None Should Perish (Regal Books) is in my opinion the
state-of-the-art exposition of how to combine high levels of
evangelism and Christian unity in reaching a city for Christ.

If I were to write a prescription for a cure to hyper-cooperativism, I would require reading *That None Should Perish*, but
in tandem with another of the finest recent books I have seen,
Primary Purpose (Creation House) by Pastor Ted Haggard of

New Life Church in Colorado Springs. Silvoso is the master strategist, and Haggard is the practical, down-to-earth local church pastor, who, out on the front lines of his own city has seen pastors come together across theological lines for the purpose of evangelizing his city. Haggard's advocacy of Christian unity is not unity as an end in itself, but unity aimed at the goal, which he uses as the subtitle of his book: *Making It Hard for People to Go to Hell from Your City!*

Notes

1. This research was reported in Win C. Arn, "A Church Growth Look at Here's Life America," *Church Growth: America* (January-February 1977): 4 ff.; and C. Peter Wagner, "Who Found It?" *Eternity* (September 1977): 13-19.
2. Lyle E. Schaller, "Reflections on Cooperative Ministries," *The Clergy Journal* (September 1977): 21.
3. Ibid.
4. Ibid.
5. Ibid.
6. Ibid.
7. Ibid.
8. Lyle E. Schaller, *The Small Membership Church* (Nashville: Abingdon Press, 1994), p. 62.

Chapter 6

KOINONITIS:
ARE WE SPIRITUAL
NAVEL-GAZERS?

Like hyper-cooperativism, koinonitis is a church disease
caused by too much of a good thing.

Koinonia is the biblical word for fellowship, a recognized
Christian virtue. The believers in that vigorous, healthy
church started in Jerusalem on the Day of Pentecost were said
to be characterized, among other things, *by koinonia* (see Acts
2:42). The apostle Paul thanks God for the Philippian believers' *"fellowship* in the gospel" (Phil. 1:5, emphasis mine). The
apostle John says that Christians who walk in the light have
"fellowship with one another" (1 John 1:7, emphasis mine).
These are just a few of the many references to Christian fellowship in the New Testament.

FELLOWSHIP IS
ESSENTIAL FOR GROWTH

Providing appropriate structures for fellowship to occur is
essential for healthy church growth. When these are either
nonexistent or when they become inoperative for some reason

or other, the church usually fails to grow. Ordinarily, when people become Christians they have choices about which church they decide to join. They may visit several churches during a period of time before they finally decide on one. In most cases, a church attracts newcomers in the first place through the worship service, especially the music. So-called "seeker-sensitive" churches have become accomplished in creating the kind of weekend event that draws visitors.

In the long haul, what matters most to those trying to find the right church for themselves is who else is attending the same church. Successful churches find a way to link people to people in more than just a casual way. For many it is done through adult Sunday School where classes of 35 to 80 people meet weekly, establish friendships and minister to one another. In others it is done through home-cell groups of 8-12, which usually meet one night a week in members' homes. Others organize the church members into ministry teams that meet regularly to accomplish a useful task. The choir is a common example of a ministry team. Others use special interest groups such as basketball leagues or women's fellowships or bowling teams to help people establish meaningful relationships.

When we interview people who might have visited a certain church for a time, but then have become members of another nearby church, the reason most frequently given is that they found fellowship, or *koinonia,* in one church but not in the other.

Recognizing, therefore, that *koinonia* is an essential feature of the life of a dynamic, healthy church is of utmost importance in understanding the growth-obstructing disease we are calling "koinonitis."

THE TWO DANGER AREAS

Two areas are related to church life in which koinonitis most frequently occurs. One could be said to involve the *quality* of the fellowship groups, and the other could be said to relate to their *quantity,* not the quantity of groups, but the number of people in each one. The first I would like to call "fellowship inflammation" and the second "fellowship saturation." Churches, whether large or small, that seem to have growth-inhibiting problems would do well to take a close look at both of these areas.

1. FELLOWSHIP INFLAMMATION

It is a well-known fact that everyone needs a certain amount of thyroid to maintain good physical health. If something happens to the thyroid gland and it begins overproducing, however, other bodily systems are thrown off, and a person's general health is in jeopardy. The same thing applies to church fellowship. *Koinonia* can easily be overdone until it becomes not just good Christian fellowship, but fellowship inflammation. As a consequence, the whole organism suffers, and the church cannot grow as it should.

Fellowship, by definition, involves interpersonal relationships. It happens when Christian believers get to know one another, to enjoy one another and to care for one another. As the disease sets in, however, and *koinonia* becomes *koinonitis*, these interpersonal relationships tend to become so deep and so mutually absorbing that they can be regarded as the central focal point for almost all church activity and involvement. When this is allowed to occur, church programs tend to become centripetal, drawing participants inward toward each other, rather than centrifugal, pushing people outward to reach others for Christ.

It is easy to understand how this happens. It takes considerable time and effort and energy to establish friendly relationships with others and to nourish them to the point where meaningful fellowship is occurring on a regular basis. Each person in a fellowship group has made a considerable personal investment in the social dynamics of the group. When their investment begins to pay off, and positive relationships become established, a protective mechanism naturally begins to build. Both clergy and laity may find themselves spending most of their church time enjoying each other in one way or another.

This is a good thing, but before anyone realizes it, the group can begin to degenerate into an exclusive circle of spiritual navel-gazers. Everyone involved feels so good about everyone else that more often than not the disease is not noticed. It is one of those silent, almost symptomless diseases, something like high blood pressure in the human. The only way patients can know they have high blood pressure before it is too late is to take the tests. If constant measurements are not taken, the problem can surreptitiously worsen until the patient suffers a stroke. It is then too late for preventative medicine

In the case of a church, the functional equivalent of a stroke is a decrease in the rate of growth, and then plateau or stag-

---

The goal is not to correct church decline; it is to maintain growth and prevent decline.

---

nation. Constant monitoring of the growth of the church and particularly of the rates of growth will provide warning signals. It will not cure the illness, but it will indicate that something needs to be done and done soon. The goal is not to correct church decline; it is to maintain growth and *prevent* decline.

Evangelistic Myopia

Churches suffering from acute fellowship inflammation do not grow as they could. This is the end result of koinonitis, although the cause and effect are often hidden to those who are enjoying the fellowship. In a surprisingly large number of cases, churches experiencing koinonitis don't really care whether they grow or not.

The reason for this is that somewhere in the process of developing the disease, the primary focus in the church's philosophy of ministry has become "us." The church has begun to exist almost exclusively for itself and for its members, as opposed to focusing its energies on those who are yet outside the fellowship. The people within the church have been reconciled to God, and they love each other. Who cares about those outside? Bible verses mentioning that some people are lost, or that God is not willing that any should perish, or that Christians are supposed to preach the gospel to every creature are acknowledged, but not frequently highlighted.

Usually it is unintended, but an evangelistic myopia, or nearsightedness, frequently develops as a symptom of koinonitis. Lost men and women are all around them, but no one in the church can "see" them, so to speak. The most important ones are the people who are saved, not those who are still unsaved. Some churches that have evangelistic myopia go as far as to develop an aversion to anything that smacks of sharing the gospel. Soul winning is considered almost abnormal Christian behavior. "Evangelism" is equated by some to proselytism, and is considered a pejorative term. Why try to win other people to Christ? We have no right to force our beliefs on them!

Church growth? It is even more threatening than evangelism to many experiencing koinonitis. I recently saw an article in a prominent Christian magazine hinting that a desire that our church would grow could be regarded as a heretical position! The article argued that "small is beautiful," and warned churches against becoming victims of a worldly growth mentality. Instead of quoting Jesus' command to "Go...and make disciples of all the nations" (Matt. 28:19), the article emphasized Jesus' statement, "Where two or three are gathered together in My name, I am there in the midst of them" (18:20).

Denial Is Common
Few believers would admit they have evangelistic myopia. Deep down, most Christians know they are supposed to have a concern for the lost, a "passion for souls." Even the article I mentioned opposing church growth finds it necessary to acknowledge the Church as an agency for proclaiming the gospel. Somehow that proclamation is not expected to result in new men and women being reconciled to God, coming into the fellowship of the church and thereby causing the church to grow.

Members of churches that have koinonitis frequently say, "We are interested in *quality*, not *quantity*." They would almost invariably point to the church in Jerusalem as a high quality church because "they continued steadfastly in the apostles' doctrine and *fellowship*, in the breaking of bread, and in prayers" (Acts 2:42, emphasis mine). Ironically, the quality of the church in Jerusalem produced an accompanying increase of quantity, for "the Lord added to the church daily those who were being saved" (v. 47). Suggesting that quality is to be sought as *opposed to* quantity is another of the defensive mechanisms used to protect the warm fellowship of a church body against potential intruders.

WHERE FELLOWSHIP INFLAMMATION FLOURISHES

Although any church from any tradition can develop koinonitis, and many do, three church traditions have a particular, almost congenital susceptibility to the kind of koinonitis I call fellowship inflammation. By this I do not mean to imply that all churches identifying with these particular traditions will inevitably show symptoms of fellowship inflammation, but churches of these kinds clearly need to be more careful about preventing it than other churches might need to be

The three kinds of churches to which I refer are: (1) holiness churches; (2) churches identifying with renewal movements, whether charismatic or traditional; and (3) churches having a higher than average sense of group consciousness.

Holiness Churches
One of the distinctives of the holiness movement, which has roots back to John Wesley, but which took on its more contemporary form toward the end of the nineteenth century, was a renewed emphasis on the biblical teachings of living pure lives, adhering to rigid lifestyle standards for avoiding sin and cultivating higher degrees of piety than were being observed in many churches of the day. Some of the better-known groups that emerged from the holiness movement were the Church of the Nazarene, the Church of God (Anderson, Indiana), the Wesleyan Church, the Salvation Army, the Free Methodist Church, the Pentecostal Holiness Church and others.

What causes many of these churches to develop koinonitis? Constant preaching and teaching about holiness frequently accomplishes its desired purpose of developing a high degree of piety among the church members in general. Their lifestyles are carefully designed to be seen as "separate from the world." A culture develops within the church that is substantially different from the surrounding culture. What is wrong with this?

It can create an excessive distance between those within the church and those outside of the church. I like to call this symptom a "sanctification gap."

The Sanctification Gap

The sanctification gap presents a dilemma because piety and sanctification are normal results of the process of Christian growth and maturity. We are all to become more Christlike. The Christian lifestyle is not to be "conformed to this world," but "transformed," we are told in Romans 12:2. Worldly habits are supposed to drop out of a Christian's life, as dead leaves fall off a tree when new life surges through in the springtime.

Although Christian behavior patterns are expected to be distinct from the world's behavior in many aspects, Christians

---

We must continue to honor sanctification and encourage piety. The way to do this and also to help close the gap is to structure the fellowship patterns of the church in such a way that it can include Christians of all stages of maturity.

---

are nevertheless urged to maintain meaningful contact with non-Christian people, communicate the gospel to them, lead them to Christ and fold those who accept the gospel into church fellowship. Witnessing to and leading unbelievers to Christ is in some ways the easier part of the process. Folding the new believers into the church can be something else again. In churches experiencing koinonitis, a new Christian can feel about as comfortable as a teenager might feel in a nursing home. A short visit is usually OK, but the residents of a nursing home would be unlikely to invite teenagers to move in with them. One experience of rock music on the stereo until midnight would quickly wear their welcome very thin.

This is analogous to the problem of churches that have developed sanctification gaps. Because the members of the church are all mature Christians, their tolerance levels for the behavior of new and immature Christians may be quite low. Although the older Christians may attempt to take steps to prevent it, their attitudes are nevertheless telegraphed in a number of ways to the new believers, and before they know it, the newcomers have evaporated. They do not feel as though they belong in such a church.

Avoiding the Sanctification Gap

How can the sanctification gap be prevented? Certainly we cannot choose the option of advocating that Christians become more worldly. The Bible would not allow this. We must continue to honor sanctification and encourage piety. The way to do this and also to help close the gap is to structure the fellowship patterns of the church in such a way that it can include Christians of all stages of maturity. Room must be made for what the Bible calls "babes in Christ." If koinonitis persists, this is virtually impossible to do because new converts can be threatening to the established fellowship patterns.

How can this happen?

If those of us who are parents recall that time when new babies first came into our homes, we can form an idea of the effect new Christians frequently have on a typical church. New babies in the home, though a blessing in one way, can also be a terrible nuisance. They yell and scream at all hours of the day and night. They show no respect for their elders. They dirty their diapers and demand to be changed. They want others to regard them as the center of attention at all times. They insist on eating, and then sometimes throw up their food. They can't be left alone, so they sharply curtail their parents' mobility. They cost money and contribute nothing economically themselves. They don't even understand what you are saying half the time. Despite these negative qualities, however, you love them, you are glad they are there, you wouldn't trade them for anything in the world—and you are also glad when they grow up.

The Lord knew that my wife and I possessed only enough parental energy to experience having babies three times. Our three girls are now grown, and the day came when we found ourselves in an empty nest. Friends warned us that when our last daughter married and left home, the "empty nest syndrome" would likely set in. True enough, ours did set in, but the best we can calculate, it lasted approximately 45 minutes! Since then we have been ecstatic. We now feel we can live the rest of our lives comfortably without more babies in the house, except perhaps for the occasional visit of a grandchild or two. It is easy to see that if my wife and I had such an attitude and if we were a church instead of a family, we would have a severe case of koinonitis!

No Price Tags on Acceptance

Church fellowship groups cannot afford to develop the feeling toward new Christians that Doris and I have toward babies. New converts should always be accepted in a church. Their behavior patterns must be tolerated. Just as babies are not born mature, neither are born-again believers mature when first converted. They will eventually grow up and develop the expected piety, but it will take time. Meanwhile, they need to feel loved and wanted. They need to know the group will require no price tags for them to be accepted. When they fall, they need to be picked up and coddled until they are ready to try again, just as when a toddler is learning to walk.

If these suggestions are put into practice, the sanctification gap cannot persist long. When a new Christian comes into the church, he or she will find many others in similar stages of discipleship with whom to identify. In a growth situation, new Christians will presumably be coming in all the time, and koinonitis will usually no longer be a problem.

When I studied the Pentecostals in Latin America some years ago, I found they had intuitively developed a workable system for avoiding the sanctification gap. One of the chief ways they make contact with new people is through open-air meetings on street corners and in the plazas.

In one church in Chile, for example, whenever people receive Christ as their Savior, they are required to appear in an open-air service the very next Sunday and give their testimonies in public. Sanctification usually has had a minimal chance to operate in their lives during one week of growth as a believer, and the unchurched people listening to them in the

open air can easily identify with the language the new converts use to tell their stories. Their unpolished delivery and
unrefined vocabulary make good sense to those who hear
them. In that church, Christians can always be found in all
stages of development, and this is one reason it has grown to
encompass more than 150,000 members, one of the largest
churches in the world.[1]

Radical Renewal Movements

During the last two or three decades, certain churches have
been profoundly influenced by renewal movements. These
have taken various forms, some featuring small groups, some
contemporary worship, some signs and wonders, some intimacy with God, some falling in the Spirit, some speaking in
tongues, some prophecy and any combination of these and
other experiences. A feature of the renewal movements has
been a rather consistent pattern of testimonies by participants
who speak of meaningful personal improvements in their
spiritual lives and in their lives in general.

An important bearer of renewal in the United States and
many other parts of the world has been the charismatic movement. Particularly those charismatic groups that have formed
within the boundaries of traditional denominations—unlike
the new apostolic church-planting networks—have a high
susceptibility to fellowship inflammation. The new experience
with the power of the Holy Spirit is so spiritually invigorating
to renewed believers that receiving it week after week
becomes an end in itself. In one way it is properly seen as an
end, but if carried to an extreme it can be likened to a dead-
end street. This has been characterized as the "bless-me syndrome."

Edward Plowman saw this coming years ago, and his
warning was timely and perhaps prophetic: "A number of
leaders are expressing concern that the main guiding forces of
the charismatic movement seem to emphasize discipleship,
teaching, and community at the expense of evangelism as a
top priority. These leaders see a specter of stagnation hovering
over the scene."[2] Through the decades, this has largely
although not exclusively been the case. Many renewal units
have self-consciously declared that their almost insatiable
desire to receive tangible blessings from God week after week

is best understood as only a temporary refreshing of the Body of Christ and a stage of preparation for aggressive evangelism, missions and church planting in the future. It has more frequently than not, however, halted with the "bless-me syndrome"—a clear symptom of koinonitis.

Dangers of Group Consciousness

Some denominations by nature have a higher group consciousness than do others. For many church members, their denominational affiliation is a vital part of their own self-identity. They could hardly imagine not being a member of their particular denomination, or of marrying someone not a member of that denomination, or even of encouraging their children to marry outside of the denomination, at least as their Plan A. If such families move from one city to another, they usually are willing to travel almost any distance on Sundays to worship in their kind of church.

The most common contributing cause for high group consciousness is a church that began with an immigrant population. Examples that come to mind are German Mennonites, Dutch Reformed, German Baptists, Scandinavian or German Lutherans, Swedish Baptists and British Salvation Army. Another cause is a radical countercultural lifestyle that may be found among such denominations as the Seventh-day Adventists. Whatever the history, churches having a high group consciousness do not find it natural to welcome strangers. Their church signs read in large letters "Visitors Welcome," but it does not take the average visitor long to find that the words have little meaning.

An interesting analysis of koinonitis in Seventh-day Adventist churches was made by one of their respected church growth scholars, Gottfried Oosterwal of Andrews University. In his book about church growth among Seventh-day Adventists, Oosterwal admits that group consciousness hinders growth in many an Adventist congregation: "New members, without an Adventist background, often do not feel at home in the church."[3]

He goes on to explain that outsiders do not naturally share the "Adventist group experience," they do not know "Adventist language" and Adventist behavior seems strange to them. Seventh-day Adventists themselves are observably counterculture. They worship on a different day, they eat different foods and they have different standards of dress than do most Anglo-Americans. This is not necessarily a weakness, but a denominational strength that both they and outsiders fully recognize. Oosterwal argues:

> All this would not be so bad—for it points to the strength of the church as a group-religion and a whole way of life—were it not for the fact that the other members of the church, reared in an Adventist community and usually unaware of the struggle of the new members, *offer them no help in this matter*.[4]

Oosterwal found that all *rapidly growing* Adventist churches have solved this problem and have become open and helpful to new members. He doesn't use the word, but the growing churches have either avoided or they have recovered from "koinonitis."

Some other churches with high group consciousness have developed it around extended families and these, too, need to be aware of the dangers of koinonitis. I have a report, for example, that in the First Christian Church of Harriman, Tennessee, out of 250 members, only 5 were not related to the others by blood or marriage. That was some years ago, and the church is now dead. Koinonitis is not necessarily terminal, but it can easily kill a church if it gets out of hand and goes too far.

2. FELLOWSHIP SATURATION

If fellowship *inflammation* and all its ramifications focus on the *manner* in which people relate to each other, fellowship *saturation* focuses on the *number* of people who relate to each other.

To understand this kind of koinonitis, it is helpful to be aware of the three basic internal structures of a church. I like to refer to these three structures as "the internal organs" of the Body of Christ. They are the *celebration*, the *congregation* and the *cell*.

The *celebration* is the membership group of the church. It usually meets on Sunday morning for worship, but it may also meet at other times. If you belong to a church, you are, de facto, part of the celebration.

The *congregation* is a fellowship group. A church may have just one, or it may have many congregations. The congregation is a group in which all the members know one another. Although there is no limit for the size of the celebration, the congregation ideally should have between 35 and 80 members.

The *cell* is the spiritual kinship group. In it, the members not only know one another, but they also share their lives with one another on a deeper level, almost as if they belonged to the same family. Interpersonal relationships are more intimate in the cell than they are in the congregation. Cell members hold themselves spiritually accountable to one another. Its ideal size is 8 to 12 members.

Folding New Members

Folding new members into the church usually takes place in the congregation or in the celebration. Here is where the newcomers usually first make friends and find their fellowship or *koinonia*. Some churches, particularly so-called cell-based churches, also use cells for folding in new people, but if so, they are specifically designed as "reproductive" cells rather than "nutritive" cells. Reproductive cells need to be intentionally designed as such to prevent koinonitis.

Koinonitis is usually not a severe growth problem in either the celebration or the cell. But in that intermediate grouping called the congregation, koinonitis can easily occur not only through the ways that have been described as fellowship inflammation, but also by becoming too large. Congregations that pass the 80 membership mark are susceptible to fellowship saturation. Congregations that are larger than 100 members are in trouble and will probably either have begun or soon will begin to plateau, if not decline.

The reason for this is directly related to the function of the group. Although fellowship groups can take several different forms, such as adult Sunday School classes, task-oriented groups, neighborhood groupings or others, the function is the same: to provide social fellowship one with another.

Why Eighty Is a Ceiling

Research has found that the average church member knows 40 to 60 other people in the church on a first-name basis, no matter whether the church has 100, 500 or 5,000 members. Part of the essential function of a congregation is for each member to know and to be known by all the others. In a group of up to 40 members, it can be done easily. In a group of more than 40, it begins to stretch. At 80, the average person will know only about 1 out of every 2 people in the group and the fellowship function is greatly diminished.

Before this ceiling is reached, attitudes frequently develop that tend to exclude outsiders. Outsiders are not excluded because they might be incompatible with the culture or lifestyle of current members; they are excluded because the fellowship dynamic of the group is already saturated and operating at a low efficiency. Many members of the congregational-sized group are already frustrated because they can't put a name on every face of the people they see fairly regularly. Newcomers only make the situation worse.

Note that fellowship saturation occurs in both small and large churches. Smaller churches may have only one fellowship group. If so, and if the fellowship group does not divide, the church itself will not grow past the so-called 200 barrier. Considering this, it is not surprising to find that a full 80 percent of American churches have 200 or fewer active members. A chief cause is koinonitis.

In larger churches that have developed many fellowship groups, however, fellowship saturation often raises a practically invisible barrier to growth. Fellowship groups or congregations should be identified and examined. If koinonitis has become a problem for any of them, it needs to be corrected on a case-to-case basis if the church is going to regain health and begin to grow.

RECOVERING FROM KOINONITIS

The cure for koinonitis is straightforward and simple: *divide*. If *fellowship inflammation* is the problem, the fellowship groups should be divided, if for nothing else than just to disturb the status quo and force some new alignments. When this happens, conscious steps need to be taken to be sure that the resulting groups are now open to outsiders and that newcomers are cared for properly. The best way to do this is to incorporate newcomers, preferably new Christians, as soon as possible.

If *fellowship saturation* is the problem, each growing congregation or subcongregation should plan to divide before the membership approaches 80. Two new groups of 35 or 40 each are plenty large enough to provide social fellowship, but small enough to avoid koinonitis. This kind of division should constitute a pattern. It should be a regular part of the church's lifestyle. If it bogs down, so will the growth of the church.

Now, I realize that the cure for koinonitis is not easy. *Koinonia* is a precious thing, and dividing groups invariably involves breaking up some existing fellowship. The mere suggestion that fellowship groups should divide will surely precipitate some negative reactions. I can think of many cures for human diseases, however, that are not pleasant either, but that we endure to be healthy once again. Church groups should have the same attitude. Groups need to divide, not for convenience, but for growth. Because dividing groups does not usually come naturally, strong pastoral leadership is frequently called for at this point. If pressure from below does not do the job, pressure from above may need to be applied.

Let's refuse to be spiritual navel-gazers. Those who take seriously the commands of our Lord to "make disciples of all nations" should be willing to pay the price and receive God's blessing in renewed church growth. In a healthy church a passion for souls will outweigh a passion for security.

Notes

1. This is described in detail in C. Peter Wagner's *Spiritual Power and Church Growth* (Orlando, Fla.: Creation House, 1986), pp. 43-45.
2. Edward E. Plowman, "The Deepening Rift in the Charismatic Movement," *Christianity Today* (October 10, 1975): 52.
3. Gottfried Oosterwal, *Patterns of SDA Church Growth in North America* (Berrien Springs, Mich.: Andrews University Press, 1976), pp. 51-52.
4. Ibid.

Chapter 7

SOCIOLOGICAL STRANGULATION: OUTGROWING THE FACILITIES

Of the nine diseases identified and described in this book, sociological strangulation is the only one that is specifically a disease of a *growing* church. This needs to be stressed up front because I have found that before some people finish reading this chapter they are trying to determine what they can do about sociological strangulation in their plateaued or declining church. They too quickly forgot that their church is not one of those susceptible to the disease.

Growing churches that wish to maintain their growth rates are those that need to be on the alert for sociological strangulation. This disease can usually be anticipated with considerable accuracy long before the symptoms are visible. I know of cases in which the warnings could be seen up to five years in advance, although relatively few churches have enough foresight to muster the courage for early action.

The term itself, "sociological strangulation," is not a new one. I have borrowed it from others who have been using it for some time. I am not entirely pleased with such a choice of words, but as with names of many of our human diseases, if it is used regularly it simply becomes part of one's vocabulary. After all, "spinal meningitis" or "diverticulitis" are not easy terms to learn, but we use them. The concept behind sociological strangulation certainly is valid, and I see no immediate reason to suggest that the terminology be changed.

POT-BOUND CHURCHES

What is sociological strangulation? It is a slowdown in the rate of church growth caused when the flow of people into a church begins to exceed the capacity of the facilities to accommodate it. In other words, a church, like a plant, can become "pot bound." If the root system becomes too big for the pot,

---

Sociological strangulation is known to affect the growth of a church in two particular danger areas: parking area and sanctuary space.

---

the plant will grow less; and as Japanese bonsai gardeners know, the resulting growth may be abnormal. This may be an interesting curiosity for gardeners, but not for churches. Healthy, vigorous church growth requires space.

Growing churches that wish to continue to grow need to keep this front and center in their planning process. Even more than with some other diseases, an ounce of prevention is worth a pound of cure. If plans to avoid sociological strangulation are not made in time and if the growth momentum falls off accordingly, the entire growth process can come to a fairly abrupt halt. If and when that happens, it is much more difficult to regain the lost momentum than it would have been to prevent the difficulty before it occurred.

The reasons for needing special courage to manage socio-logical strangulation are: (a) facility needs often cannot be handled immediately, and (b) usually a substantial budgetary provision is necessary to take care of the situation. Few congregations can be motivated to take aggressive budgetary action unless they have an emergency. The purpose of the kind of planning I am suggesting is to *avoid* an emergency, but that is not always easy to communicate. Blessed is the church that has the leadership capable of motivating *preventive* action, rather than just *therapeutic* action.

THE DANGER AREAS

Sociological strangulation is known to affect the growth of a church in two particular danger areas: *parking area* and *sanctuary space*.

The disease can be caused by other facility problems to be sure; but those that relate to other than parking and sanctuary issues are usually more specific to a certain philosophy of ministry. For example, if adult Sunday School is a vital part of the activities of the church, Christian education facilities become very important. Churches that are targeting young suburban married couples will not grow well without adequate quality nursery facilities. Church planners know that parking and sanctuary considerations apply to churches across the board more than any other considerations. Let's discuss them one at a time.

PARKING

Robert Schuller, in his book *Your Church Has a Fantastic Future*,[1] includes a fascinating chapter entitled "Seven Principles of Successful Retailing." Although many theologians decry the application of marketing techniques to the church, Robert Schuller was one of the first to be bold enough to say that churches really should see themselves in the business of retailing religion. I want to agree with both sides. Many manipulative features of secular marketing should not be adopted by Christians. On the other hand, it makes a great deal of common sense to understand churches as analogous to retailers. Interpreting God's will and His kingdom to the general public is the task of the local church. A Christian friend of mine who is in the advertising business says, "Sell it like it is."

Schuller's principle of successful retailing relating to sociological strangulation is "surplus parking." Understanding the importance of this is, in America, basically a cultural matter. Lack of parking would not be a deterrent to church growth among the Danis of Irian Jaya or the fishing people of Bangladesh. For most of contemporary America, however, the use of the automobile is a central cultural value. Whether it *ought* to be that way or not might provide a good topic for a debating society or for Christian social ethicists. Until the matter is resolved to the satisfaction of all, however, the fact remains that large numbers of American people, whom our churches are responsible for winning to Jesus Christ, do consider their automobiles an essential part of their lifestyles. Wheels are regarded as a necessity of life, along with food, clothing and housing.

Of course, there are some exceptions. Automobiles could be considered an unnecessary burden for some living on Manhattan Island, for example. But in relatively few areas across the country would such a case be true. Large numbers of Americans use their cars when they have to go just three or four blocks to buy a newspaper or pick up a child. They use their cars for grocery shopping, for transportation to work, to go out for an evening or to visit friends. Successful shopping centers, athletic stadiums, libraries, colleges and amusement parks all plan far in advance for surplus parking. They have learned that when the average American finds a parking lot full, or so nearly full that it is difficult to find a place to park, he or she is not likely to return to that place frequently. This is an important lesson for churches as well.

Empty Parking Spaces

The church parking lot should have *empty* parking spaces during the peak traffic times at the Sunday morning worship services. This is the chief test for potential sociological strangulation. If the parking lot is full during the main service, the church is already losing potential new members. It is a sign that evangelistic effectiveness probably has peaked and is beginning to diminish.

In most cases, faithful members and Christian workers are

accustomed to arriving at church early, and they choose the best spaces in the parking lot. Well before the service begins, the prime spaces have been occupied by the Sunday School teachers, the deacons, the choir members and the ushers. Furthermore, they often occupy these spaces from the beginning of the Sunday morning activities until the end, including during multiple services.

Strangers and visitors customarily arrive about five minutes before the worship service starts. If they find the parking lot full and have to drive around the streets, walk some distance to get from their cars to the church and arrive late for the worship service, the whole experience might prove to be too much for them. They may not be in the mood to appreciate even the best of worship services, choir presentations or biblical messages. Many will make plans to go elsewhere next Sunday. Others may decide they can find something better to do than going to church on Sunday morning if it involves that much hassle.

Worse yet, the church leaders almost never discover this directly. If a long-time church member decides to leave, everyone will likely know about it and know the reasons. Their friends will spread the word even if the member decides not to let the pastor know directly. Visitors and casual attenders do not yet have a circle of friends in the church, however, and when they decide to go elsewhere they just disappear and no one is the wiser. This is why it is necessary to take the test: count the empty spaces in the parking lot, and *assume* that losses are occurring if no empty spaces can be found.

Solving the Parking Problem

Curing the disease of sociological strangulation caused by inadequate parking can be accomplished in three ways. One is to vacate choice parking spaces and reserve them for visitors, another is to acquire new land and a third is to park at a distance.

Although it is not a long-term solution to the problem, immediate steps can be taken in almost any church to vacate choice parking spaces and reserve them for visitors. A volunteer team of parking attendants can help greatly. Just the fact that some attendants, dressed in bright orange vests, are in the lot is impressive to those who are visiting the church. A sign at the entrance instructing visitors to turn on their headlights also helps the process. The added excitement is usually good public relations.

The most obvious long-term solution to the problem is to purchase adjoining land and expand the parking facilities to accommodate those who want to use them. City zoning ordinances usually require the provision of adequate parking when new facilities are first built. If present facilities are already overcrowded, however, it will ordinarily affect the parking.

A problem for many urban churches is the inflated value of real estate in the immediate vicinity of the church. Many churches purchased their first property at $10 to $20 thousand an acre, only to be faced with $80 to $100 thousand an acre or more for additional parking. This is one reason many churches now are looking for 15 to 20 acres or more to begin with when purchasing new sanctuary sites. The extremely high cost of multiple-level parking garages has been found almost universally prohibitive for churches.

Parking at a Distance
An alternative way to handle the problem of inadequate parking is to require, to the extent possible, that church members leave home early and park at a distance from the church. Some can find curbside parking several blocks away from the church and walk the distance to the church. The Sunday morning use of nearby off-street parking lots can often be negotiated with businesses, shopping centers or restaurants in the vicinity. If these parking lots are distant, shuttle-bus services can be provided to transport members to and from the church campus.

It is not always easy to convince members that they should implement the new parking plan, and once begun, it is not always easy to enforce. A high degree of *esprit de corps* has to exist among the members, and it has to be seen as a substantial contribution to the overall mission of the church in the community, and to the health of the church.

I recall some time ago the pastor of our own church requested that members of our church were to park at a distance to leave ample parking for the elderly, handicapped, marginal attendees and visitors. Some did for a while, but soon many otherwise faithful members were once again unashamedly taking up space in the parking lot during peak times on Sunday mornings.

Through this period, the church was growing (although not as much as it should have grown) and the situation soon became more acute than ever. This time the church leased a parking structure four blocks away and installed a shuttle bus service running every few minutes. The whole process received a great deal of publicity and when it began, hundreds of people used the shuttle service, attendance remained stable and the shuttle system has been a part of church life ever since.

THE SANCTUARY

The seating capacity of the sanctuary is the second danger area, perhaps more critical than lack of parking. As a rule of thumb, when the church is growing and sanctuary seating is 80 percent full, you can expect that sociological strangulation has already begun to set in. Growth rates will almost invariably begin to drop at that point. Although you may not see it, you are already losing members, and the members you are losing are not the old faithful. They will usually hang in there week in and week out even though they complain about a crowded sanctuary. Unfortunately, the members you are losing are mostly the newcomers, trying your church a time or two, but somehow not feeling comfortable during their visits.

If the church is otherwise healthy, it might keep on growing as the 80 percent point is passed. Church growth is complex and several areas of strength can outweigh some areas of weakness for a time. But if the 80 percent principle is violated, the annual rate will usually become slower and slower. In any case, it is almost certain that the church that has an over-crowded sanctuary is not growing as fast as it would if there were more space.

Temporary, stop-gap measures can and should be put into place. In almost any church, ushers can be trained to see that all seats are filled without excessively inconveniencing the attenders. Until the fire marshal decides to take action, some churches can provide additional seating by placing chairs in the aisles, using the stairways as seats and even by sitting on the floor. Others can utilize overflow auditoriums by providing closed-circuit television. Plans should be made, however, to replace these temporary measures by providing better seating as soon as possible. If the church is growing well, such auxiliary provisions will soon be at capacity themselves and growth will once again be choked off.

Three major long-term options for curing this kind of sociological strangulation can be implemented. Depending on the local circumstances, at least one of the three should definitely become part of the long-range church planning well before attendance in the present sanctuary reaches the 80 percent capacity level. A simple growth graph of the last two or three years, projected to the future, will provide an immediate reading of approximately when the 80 percent figure might be reached, thus avoiding the element of being taken by surprise.

Add Another Service

The first and invariably the most economical option is to add another Sunday worship service. Going from one service to two immediately doubles the seating capacity of the sanctuary and requires no capital investment.

The mathematics of this decision is quite a bit easier than it is to persuade some people in the church that it should happen. In almost every case, when the pastor first suggests to the lay church leadership that the church should plan two services, someone will say, "Oh no, pastor! We can't do that! If we go to two services we will become two churches!" This kind of statement is a sure symptom of koinonitis! For a church to grow, one of the things it ordinarily needs the most is to divide the fellowship group, but some members will continue to value their fellowship more than taking the necessary steps to reach new people. In such cases, koinonitis needs to be treated before sociological strangulation can properly be managed.

A Checklist for Multiple Services

Once the church has decided to start a second service, several items should be considered as part of the planning:

• The timing of the services should ensure that the parking lot can be emptied and refilled between services. Facilitating this is another reason for recruiting a team of volunteer parking lot attendants.

• Should the services be identical or should one be contemporary and the other traditional? There is no standard answer to this question. The services must fit the philosophy of ministry of the church, and be tailored for the target audiences.

If the services are to be identical, uniform quality needs to be maintained to attract reasonably equal numbers of people to each service. For example, if a sanctuary choir is an important part of the worship experience, the choir should perform in both services, usually leaving the second service right after singing the anthem. Using a junior choir of some kind in the second service has not usually proved successful.

It is common these days for a traditional church to consider adding a contemporary service as the second service to reach younger families in the community. An increasing number of churches are choosing Saturday night for this purpose, although the earlier Sunday service is also appropriate for such a format. Experience has shown that the primary factor contributing to the success or failure of the contemporary service is the music. The more traditional ministers of music are not always versatile enough to handle both music styles, and many churches have found it worthwhile to add to the staff a specialist in contemporary worship for the contemporary service to succeed as it should.

Whether identical or alternative services, ordinarily the pastor preaches the same sermon in both, perhaps using cosmetic adaptations. This is important from the perspective of maintaining the overall leadership and cohesion of the church.

• If Sunday School is a significant component of the philosophy of ministry of the church, the church will have to decide whether to have one Sunday School session, usually between the two worship services, or whether to offer two Sunday School sessions simultaneous with the worship services. From the viewpoint of time and convenience, particularly if the Sunday School is offered mainly for children, two Sunday School sessions are preferable. The staff of Sunday School teachers and superintendents, however, will have to be doubled to accomplish this. Some see this as a plus because it can open more ministry opportunities for laypeople desiring to serve the Lord.

If adult classes are important, they can be offered simultaneously with each worship service. Adults will then have the choice of attending worship services or Sunday School classes.

Although a Sunday School scheduled between the two services has some advantages, especially in terms of requiring less volunteer personnel, it can also tax the facilities and add to the problem of sociological strangulation. It obviously requires up to double the classroom space than it would to offer two Sunday Schools. It also produces two times per morning the situation in which automobiles are leaving and entering the parking areas simultaneously instead of the usual one.

• How about starting a third service? The energy and adjustment required to go from one service to two can be handled by most churches, although there are some exceptions as we will see. Adding a third service as a part of long-range planning, however, is almost a quantum leap. Many pastors who can handle two services fairly well find that they do not have the additional energy reserves to sustain three. If the third service is seen as only a stop-gap measure, more pastors can handle it. If the third service is held on Saturday night, the pastor's energy level seems to be less of an inhibiting factor.

Exceptions to the Rule

• I mentioned earlier that there may be some exceptions to the rule of offering two services on Sunday morning as a viable first-choice option for curing sociological strangulation. This is largely a function of the church's particular philosophy of ministry.

Some worship styles virtually exclude the possibility of duplicate services. Generally speaking, a worship format that requires an extraordinarily high level of emotional output from the preacher cannot easily be duplicated. Perhaps the majority of black churches and many Southern white Pentecostal churches, for example, find themselves in this position. In those churches that have a strong vocal audience response to what the preacher says, the energy output of both preacher and congregation during a single sermon is enormous. By the time many such preachers finish their sermons, they are drained, both physically and emotionally. Typically, they are no more capable of repeating the effort than a professional basketball team is capable of playing a doubleheader.

Other philosophies of ministry, however, demand an energy output more analogous to a baseball game. Most baseball players, with the exception of the pitcher, and sometimes the catcher, are able to play doubleheaders. The energy output is considerably lower than it is in basketball.

Traditional non-Pentecostal Anglo-American preachers have been trained to use large amounts of their energy during the week while *preparing* their Sunday sermons. By the time they enter the pulpit, they are ready to speak from extended

---

The more sedate and liturgical a church's worship services are, the higher possibility it has for curing sociological strangulation by starting multiple services.

---

notes or a manuscript or sometimes from rote memory. Some of them still preach by using a good deal of expression and movement, but compared to African-American and Southern Pentecostal preachers, the spontaneous energy level is minimal. When using good principles of larynx control so that the voice doesn't tire, this kind of preaching can be repeated two or three times on a Sunday morning and can be expected to have a similar effect on the congregation each time.

The more sedate and liturgical a church's worship services are, the higher possibility it has for curing sociological strangulation by starting multiple services.

It may occur to some churches that a variation of this option might be to have different staff members preach at different Sunday morning services. This is being done with good results in some churches; however, such cases are unusual. Unless a church has a special growth mix that will permit this to happen and still allow the church membership to increase, it should not be regarded as a significant possibility. The senior pastor of the church is the number one key to its growth, and the pastor's major role is to provide leadership for the congregation. This leadership is usually projected in a uniquely important way through the Sunday sermon. For this reason, church growth pastors will not often relinquish their pulpits.

Build a Larger Sanctuary

The second option for solving the problem of sanctuary capacity is to build a larger one. This is such an obvious route that it hardly needs comment. A chief factor in the decision to build a new sanctuary is, of course, money. Walking the fine line between faith and presumption is a challenge for any pastor or church leader. How far do we stretch our faith and believe that the future growth will pay the bills?

Just announcing plans for a new sanctuary can often cause enough excitement, anticipation and hope to turn around a decreasing growth rate. The world's largest church, the Yoido Full Gospel Church of Seoul, Korea, found it had sociological strangulation when its membership reached 8,000, but its sanctuary seated only 2,000. The decadal growth rate had dropped to only 27 percent, the lowest it had ever been. Then Pastor David Yonggi Cho announced that he was going to build a sanctuary seating 10,000. During the next three years, while the building was still being constructed, the decadal growth rate went up to 308 percent. Then, when the $5 million building was dedicated and put to use, the rate went up to an amazing 1,155 percent per decade. This was back in the 1970s, and within the next 20 years the membership had reached 700,000. Part way during the process another case of sociological strangulation set in and Pastor Cho had to expand the 10,000 seat sanctuary to 25,000 seats.

As I have said, new sanctuary construction is but one of the several options for curing sociological strangulation. Before a church decides to go this route, it is often wise to employ a knowledgeable church growth consultant to examine the dynamics and the advisability of investing in a new sanctuary.

Growth by Division

Whenever a sanctuary begins to reach capacity, another option frequently comes to mind. How about splitting off a segment of our church and forming the nucleus for a new church plant? That will solve our problem of overcrowding, and also provide a new church that will have great growth potential of its own for our community.

For many reasons, this solution is the most ideal of all. As far as a strategic design is concerned, constantly spinning off church planting groups has the greatest evangelistic influence possible on the community. As I have said many times, planting new churches is the most effective evangelistic method under heaven! Five healthy new churches bring many more people to Christ and is much more cost effective than any church building program could possibly provide.

Having said that, new church planting also has a serious downside. This is such a good idea that it has been experimented with many times. The jury is now in and the conclusion is clear. Churches that have attempted to use growth by division as a cure for sociological strangulation have typically been able to establish the first new church without much difficulty. The second new church is more of an effort. By the time the third church is planted, little energy remains for doing it again.

As a general rule, after three church plants at the most, plans change. For one thing, God usually blesses these innovative churches so much that their vacated spaces fill up much faster than anticipated. Therefore, the effort hasn't helped sociological strangulation very much. The morale of many church members also suffers greatly when they continually have to bid farewell to their friends who are leaving for new churches. It is easy to underestimate the corporate expenditure or energy required to hive off a new church.

Although growth by division is a superb idea, I cannot guarantee it as a practical, long-range cure for sociological strangulation.

AVOIDING EXTREMES

Is it possible to have too much vacant space in the parking lot and in the worship center? Obviously it is, and vacant space can then become a psychological deterrent to growth.

It is a good rule to make your church parking lot seem as full and well used as possible. A friend of mine was pastoring a small Presbyterian church in Georgia that wouldn't grow. He had studied church growth, but he could not seem to identify the reasons more people weren't coming to the church.

The breakthrough came when a new family joined the church and was later conversing with the pastor. They told him that after they had moved into their home, they had set out to attend his Presbyterian church one Sunday, but when they saw only five cars in the parking lot, they thought they had missed the service and they went to the Methodist church instead. They looked at the Presbyterian church again the next Sunday and thought that the children's Sunday School might be in session and the service would come later, so they tried the Baptist church that day. Being persistent, they made some telephone calls and found that the Presbyterian service indeed was being held at the normal time.

That was all my pastor friend needed to know. The next Sunday he shared the family's story with his congregation and said, "Now I know how our church can grow. Some of you have more than one car in your family. If you do, starting next Sunday, please bring all your cars to church when you come and park them toward the front of the parking lot!" The people in his congregation did what he said, and he showed me the growth graph of the church taking a decided upswing starting on that next Sunday. By the time he shared the story with me, the church had been growing so much that my friend was making plans for a new sanctuary and parking lot!

Although I have not seen as much research about this as I have about the 80 percent principle, my best estimate is that a sanctuary should never have less than 50 percent occupancy. If the chairs are movable, it is a simple matter to keep the seating to proportion. If the sanctuary contains pews, I would advise removing enough pews from the sanctuary to attain 50 percent occupancy. The pews can easily be stored and moved back when necessary. Meanwhile, a minimal amount of interior decoration can provide the half-empty worship center with a warm and attractive environment.

Note
1. Robert H. Schuller, *Your Church Has a Fantastic Future* (Ventura, Calif.: Regal Books, 1974; revised edition, 1986), pp. 246-248.

Chapter 8

ARRESTED SPIRITUAL DEVELOPMENT: WE SHOULD BE ACTING OUR AGE!

Human beings whose growth is retarded are often victims of arrested physical development. A gland or a digestive malfunction or nerve damage might cause this. A recent news item told of an extreme case of child abuse, in which a seven-year-old girl was discovered in a small closet where her parents had kept her all her life. She couldn't walk, she had learned to say only a few words and she weighed less than 40 pounds. Hers was a pathetic case of arrested physical development. She probably will never be normal.

The causes for nongrowth in many churches can be traced to spiritual conditions that are parallel to the kind of arrested physical development as was experienced by the seven-year-old girl. When people in the church are not growing in the things of God or in their relationships with one another, the total health of the church deteriorates, and the church cannot grow.

Arrested spiritual development is a problem connected with internal growth, sometimes referred to as "quality growth." If the truth were known, this might well be the most prevalent growth-obstructing disease in American churches. A church that is just barely limping along, implementing a program, raising a budget, hiring a preacher, conducting worship services and doing whatever else churches are "supposed" to do, can just be "playing church." Merely going through the motions is a ministry that will not have a significant influence on a community. Unfortunately, however, it does describe many churches in America.

Arrested spiritual development is definitely a curable disease. The first step toward therapy is to understand the problem and some of its ramifications. Once it is understood, ways and means can be found to correct such problems through biblical teaching, the guidance of other Christians and the leadership of the Holy Spirit.

A LOW REGENERATION LEVEL

In some cases, arrested spiritual development is caused by a low percentage of church members who have been born again by the power of God. Only the Lord knows how many church members have not made a personal commitment to Jesus Christ. He controls the Lamb's Book of Life, and He gives none of us access to it. Unquestionably, some church members, including some active church members, have never been personally reconciled to God through Jesus Christ.

Some churches are more susceptible to this noncommitted situation than are others. Some people join a church much as they would join a social club. They need activity of some kind. They want to build relationships. The people in church are friendly, the worship services are pleasant and the sermons are interesting. Their children can meet the right kind of friends, and being a church member is very acceptable in American society. People who have joined the church for these and other similar reasons are present in almost all churches of any denomination. As Eddie Gibbs says, "The preaching to which they have been exposed has consisted of moral homilies rather than a radical Gospel of repentance and the offer of new life in Christ."[1]

Across America, statistics show that many people belong to churches, consider themselves active members and attend church without being born again. Although slight variations exist in the figures from poll to poll, the religious profile of American adults has held fairly steady for a generation. It looks something like this:

Church members	68%
Active church members	56%
Attend church regularly	42%
Born again	36%
Evangelicals	32%

The "born-again" category may be low, according to some researchers, because certain people don't use the term or understand what it means. Some prefer the term "committed to Christ." Some prefer to be called "faithful Christians." Even if the figure were adjusted to compensate for the term differences, still tens of millions of Americans belong to a church, and even are active in a church, but have not been made "new creatures" in Christ Jesus (see 2 Cor. 5:17). All of them are in need of E-0 evangelism, leading people to Christ who are already church members.

Churches that include a high percentage of noncommitted members will suffer from arrested spiritual development. They cannot grow normally because, spiritually speaking, they have not yet been born. The people may be church members, but they are not members of the family of God, nor will they be, until they are born again. The answer to such a situation, obviously, is to lead these church members to full commitment to Jesus Christ.

SPECIALISTS IN E-0 EVANGELISM

Some people have become specialists in the field of E-0 evangelism. For example, some pastors I know believe they have a special gift and calling for E-0 evangelism. They will purposely accept a call to a church that realizes it is suffering from arrested spiritual development and wants to be healed. Those who have these gifts love to share Christ with people who may have thought they always had been Christians just because they were church members.

I recall that one friend of mine, John McClure, who now pastors a Vineyard Church, led 150 church members to a personal commitment to Christ during his first year in a new pastorate in a Congregational church. Then he began to teach them spiritual things, and they matured rapidly. For years and years, the church had not grown. The cure took a couple of years, during which time they *lost* some members who were not yet ready to see their church as anything more than a social circle. Arrested spiritual development, however, soon became a thing of the past, spiritual health began to flow through the congregation and the church moved into a vigorous growth mode. If American churches had a few thousand more pastors such as John McClure who have hearts for ministering to sick churches, America would not be far from revival.

A LOW NURTURE LEVEL

A large percentage of uncommitted Christians in a church is one form of arrested spiritual development. Another, more prevalent, form is a low level of spiritual nurture among people whose names are already written in the Lamb's Book of Life.

In 1 Corinthians 3:1,2, the apostle Paul refers to the Christians in Corinth as "babes in Christ." He is disappointed in them because he said he could not feed them solid food, but like babies, they could take only milk. Now, milk is good. The human race could not be propagated without it, and the Christian Church needs spiritual milk as well. New Christians need to be fed the milk of the Word. If they do not receive it, they will also be susceptible to arrested spiritual development and fail to mature properly. The milk, however, is not intended to be a permanent diet. Parents, as soon as possible, move their children from milk to solid food.

Pastors and other church leaders should see themselves as spiritual parents who desire that their people move from the simple things of the faith to deeper commitment and active ministry in the kingdom of God. Sadly, the members of many American churches are the equivalent of adults still on a milk diet.

MEASURING SPIRITUAL MATURITY

A routine part of the diagnosis of the health of a church should be to examine the spiritual maturity of the members. How to measure this objectively is another question. Through the years, the research method for measuring and evaluating the quantitative side of church growth has been straightforward. Measuring quality, however, has been more elusive.

One of the best efforts at identifying the chief qualities of a church has been made by the Evangelistic Association of New England and reported in a booklet, "Ten Characteristics of a Healthy Church." Their list includes God-exalting worship, God's empowering presence, an outward focus, servant-leadership development, a commitment to loving/caring relationships, learning and growing in community, personal disciplines, stewardship and generosity, wise administration and accountability, and networking with the regional church.[2] The Association has also developed a diagnostic tool designed to measure the degree to which a local church is living up to the 10 ideals. At this writing, the tool is so new that reports about its overall usefulness have not been compiled. Nevertheless, this is the kind of diagnosis that needs to be done more if we are to monitor arrested spiritual development in any helpful way.

One of the inherent problems in attempting to measure church quality is the variation of characteristics from church to church or denomination to denomination that seem to be of utmost importance to them for evaluating congregational quality. For some it is baptism or even the mode of baptism; for some it is a second blessing or sanctification; for some it is a baptism of the Holy Spirit validated by speaking in tongues; for some it is social activism, for some it is the Eucharist; for some it is participation in prayer meetings; and for others it is Sunday School attendance. All of these characteristics might be seen as good things, but none of them would be acknowledged by denominations *across the board* as important measurements for high quality of a church.

Keeping this in mind, I have chosen eight church qualities I think will apply, not entirely, but more or less to churches of any tradition. This can be used as a diagnostic checklist if you suspect that the growth of your church might be retarded by arrested spiritual development.

PHILOSOPHY OF MINISTRY

Having a well-articulated philosophy of ministry is a sign of strength in a church. The phrase "philosophy of ministry" has not been a common one among church leaders until recently. Few of us learned much about it in seminary. For a time it was thought that churches should be as much *alike* as possible, not as *distinct* from other churches as possible.

Now, however, church leaders are beginning to agree that because unchurched people are so different and have such diverse sets of needs, churches that represent a wide spectrum of philosophies of ministry are able to reach more people and meet more human needs. Thus, many churches are now attempting to think through and articulate their particular philosophy of ministry so that, first of all, their own people understand what makes their church different from others, and so that the general public begins to perceive it as well.

Some time ago, my friend Dan Baumann decided to attach some names to various philosophies of ministry he had been observing. He distinguishes, for example, between "soul-winning" churches, "life-situation" churches, "classroom" churches, "social action" churches and "general practitioner" churches. This list certainly does not exhaust the possibilities for varying philosophies of ministry, but I like the names because they are self-explanatory. The point is that each one of these churches requires a certain kind of pastor who can lead the congregation in developing a certain kind of program, and therefore will attract a certain kind of people. Few pastors would have enough professional versatility to lead more than one of these kinds of churches.

Although each of these churches would affirm that their philosophy of ministry is biblically valid and that by following it they are being faithful to God and obedient to His purposes for them, if they are mature, they will respect other churches that have developed contrasting philosophies of ministry. This seems to me to be a healthy attitude for the Body of Christ as a whole.

The philosophy of ministry, sometimes called a "mission statement," should be formulated first by the church leadership, but then it must be clearly communicated to the entire congregation. Church members who are unsure of the purpose of their church can contribute to arrested spiritual development. To avoid this, many churches include their philosophy of ministry as an important component of the curriculum of new members' classes. Communication helps to reduce it to a catchy slogan that appears again and again in print and from the pulpit. Each regular member should be indoctrinated and able to verbalize the church's particular sense of mission to anyone who might ask.

PASTORAL LEADERSHIP

As I have mentioned from time to time, the pastor of the church is the key person for determining the condition of the health and the growth of the congregation. Although it is a mistake for the pastor to attempt to do all the ministry of the church, he or she must take the responsibility of seeing that the ministry is done and that the people are taken care of somehow. The biblical analogy is that of a shepherd and the sheep. Some pastors wisely choose to be "ranchers" rather than shepherds, but they make sure that a sufficient number of shepherds are also at work caring for the needs of the sheep.

Christian people need counsel, exhortation, guidance in their lives and support during periods of crisis. If the people in the church are not receiving these things, their spiritual development will tend to be retarded. Church membership can become superficial. The function of the church in the minds of the people may become more and more divorced from real life.

The crucial role of the pastor is that of supplying leadership and vision. The pastor, more than anyone else in the church, needs to know where God wants the church to go, and needs to be able to communicate its philosophy of ministry to the members along with the steps necessary to get the church to achieve its goals.

Churches that are in the habit of changing pastors every three to six years will usually be deprived of this kind of ongoing visionary pastoral leadership, and they will suffer the consequences. As Lyle Schaller has found: "There is overwhelmingly persuasive evidence that from a long-term congregational perspective, the most productive years of a pastorate seldom *begin* before the fourth or fifth or sixth year of a minister's tenure in that congregation."[3]

Almost any minister can baptize, marry and bury, and preach acceptable sermons on Sunday mornings. If the church is interested in long-range health and vigorous growth, however, it needs to get away from the rapid turnover of ministers characteristic of so many denominations and decide to call a pastor and follow that person's leadership for an extended time period.

Faith without works is dead, as the Bible affirms, but the order must be faith and then works, not the reverse.

The degree to which the pastor can be regarded as a strong leader as opposed to a mere employee of the church members, the greater will be the potential for curing arrested spiritual development. The other alternative is a program-maintaining status quo and minimal influence on the community.

STRONG BIBLICAL CONVICTION

Throughout Christian history, the Word of God, the Bible, has been considered the main staple of the Christian's spiritual diet. Although I identify with those who emphasize that Bible *knowledge* without biblical *behavior* is next to worthless, nevertheless, it is necessary to realize that knowing God's will must *precede* the good Christian deeds. Faith without works is dead, as the Bible affirms (see Jas. 2:17), but the order must be faith and then works, not the reverse.

Christian faith is built through studying and applying God's Word. Mature Christians know the Bible, and it is central in their lives. Churches that have a "classroom" philosophy of ministry stress this more heavily than most. Typical Sunday sermons in such churches are 45- to 50-minute Bible lectures, and the members seem to thrive on them. Every church, however, whether it is a classroom church or not, needs to make sure that somehow or other its members continue to learn more and more about the Bible and develop strong biblical faith.

Many of our contemporary American churches are suffering from serious cases of arrested spiritual development because they are biblically illiterate and theologically unconcerned. A whole generation of pastors did not learn how to develop strong theological convictions in seminary. On the contrary, they were trained to believe that theological convictions are something to be avoided. The ecumenical movement, a spirit of theological pluralism, and a false sense of "theological correctness" to accompany "political correctness" have contributed to theological anemia in many churches, particularly those of the old-line denominations.

Years ago, Dean Kelley, a respected ecumenical leader, warned against this. His seminal research indicated that churches with high levels of theological conviction had more social strength, and therefore grew more vigorously, than churches with less theological conviction. He calls theological conviction "strictness," and concludes: "A group with evidences of social strength will proportionately show traits of strictness; a group with traits of leniency will proportionately show evidences of social weakness rather than strength," and he went on to say that this hypothesis "provides an explanation...for the decline of ecumenical religious societies and the continuing vitality of nonecumenical bodies in the country at this time."[4]

As might be expected, Dean Kelley received considerable criticism from his friends in the old-line denominations when his views were first made known. Signs reveal, however, that some are now breaking out of their extended period of denial and admitting that lack of theological conviction can and indeed does weaken churches. Professor Thomas Oden of Drew University, for one, has been outspoken in his criticism of theological weakness. He observes that "much of what has been studied in liberated religion under the heading of 'theology' has nothing whatsoever to do with God or God's revelation of God's church or the worship of God."[5] This leads to a situation in some of our churches and seminaries in which there is no distinction between true faith and falsehood. Oden says that in some seminaries "No heresy of any kind any longer exists....Not only is there no concept of heresy, but also there is no way even to raise the question of where the boundaries of legitimate Christian belief lie."[6]

Unless this sad state of affairs is corrected, there is little hope that many suffering churches will ever recover from arrested spiritual development.

PERSONAL PIETY AND SPIRITUAL FORMATION

An intimate walk with God as a personal dimension in the life of each Christian is of utmost importance. Regular time alone with God in prayer and in personal study of God's Word builds Christians and helps them in their spiritual formation. Although some like to structure this more than others, in one way or another, it must take place. Church members need to be taught how to improve their walk with God.

This relationship with God is an aspect of church life that is hard to gauge. Perhaps satisfactory measuring instruments will be developed someday, but I have not yet seen any. Personalities differ so much that it is usually not possible to expect people to fit into a mold in their personal preferences of how they relate to God. Some churches structure this as a part of their philosophy of ministry and insist on so much time per day in personal devotions. This can be a source of strength in the church.

Other churches are not as strict in this respect. Still others seem to think that any mention of it at all is regarded as an invasion of personal privacy. In such a case, there is not much hope for recovery from arrested spiritual development.

SPIRITUAL GIFTS

Although teaching about spiritual gifts has been increasing across America during the few past decades, ignorance of spiritual gifts is still prevalent in many churches. This ignorance is frequently a major contributing factor to arrested spiritual development.

Christians should understand that they are members of a Body—the Body of Christ. God has placed each of the members in the Body as it has pleased Him (see 1 Cor. 12:18). Being a bodily member signifies having been assigned a certain function; thus, when Christians discover their spiritual gifts, they are then able to understand what their primary function in the Body might be. Upon discovering the gift or gifts they possess, they find that God provides a supernatural kind of power in using them for His glory and for the benefit of the whole Body.

When the members know their gifts and are ministering with them, the whole tone of the church improves. It reduces envy and jealousy to a minimum. It mobilizes the membership for the various tasks of the church to maximum efficiency. It removes unnecessary guilt and helps people understand why they can do some things easily and well but not others. It brings joy and fulfillment to individuals. All this is reflected in the general atmosphere of the church and is quickly detected by newcomers.

Growing in the use of spiritual gifts is one of the most readily available cures for arrested spiritual development. Excellent tools for making this happen have been developed and tested. My book *Your Spiritual Gifts Can Help Your Church Grow* has more than 200,000 copies in circulation and has helped many believers overcome arrested spiritual development. An accompanying reproducible study guide makes it easy for pastors, Sunday School teachers and small-group leaders to teach their people how to discover their spiritual gifts and begin to minister with them and be a blessing to others.[7]

FELLOWSHIP STRUCTURES

I raised the issue of church fellowship structures in the chapter about koinonitis (chapter 6). Koinonitis is the disease that occurs when fellowship is *overdone* and becomes totally self-centered. Arrested spiritual development can occur when fellowship is *underdone*.

An essential part of being a Christian and a member of the Body of Christ is developing relationships with other Christians. Many churches do not grow because they do not satisfy the deep need for meaningful fellowship that men and women have, and that they expect to see fulfilled when they join a church. Fellowship is a crucial key to assimilating new members.

The two structures in which fellowship happens best are the congregation and the cell, as we have defined them previously. Congregations, which have 35 to 80 members, are able to promote meaningful social fellowship. Members of the group get to know one another, to know one another's families, to know their vocational involvements, to enjoy mutual interests together and to share the joys and sorrows of

All worship services have a common objective: those who worship must meet God, and His presence must be real to them as individuals and in the group.

major milestones of life. The cells, which have 8 to 12 members, serve to develop a deeper level of intimacy and mutual accountability. In them, a great deal of caring can take place, thus relieving the professional staff of some routine pastoral duties.

In their book *Rekindling the Flame*, William Willimon and Robert Wilson offer strategies for restoring health to ailing United Methodist churches, many of which are suffering from arrested spiritual development. A recurring theme of the book is urging Methodists to get back to the roots established by their founder, John Wesley. Wesley, they point out, formed his people into congregations, which he called "societies," and cells, which he called "classes." The authors comment: "The formation of these small groups was the organizational stroke of genius of Methodism. Not content simply to gain enthusiastic converts who could point to some vague emotional experience as the source of their discipleship, Wesley organized people into a structure whereby they received the support, correction, and encouragement they needed to live as Christians."[8]

It couldn't be said better. Churches today that are languishing would do well to follow the lead of John Wesley and allow their people to be discipled in dynamic structures of subgroups in the church.

WORSHIP

All churches conduct worship services, but not all churches worship well. Having said this, I need to add that there is no one standard way to worship well. Differing philosophies of ministry demand different styles of worship experiences. All worship services, however, have a common objective: those who worship must meet God, and His presence must be real to them as individuals and in the group.

In all too many churches this common objective does not happen. The Sunday morning service is something that must be endured rather than enjoyed. I must confess that in various periods of my life, I would take a good book to church on Sunday morning and read it on my lap during the service. It was more enjoyable than what was going on around me. I am happy to say that I no longer do that. I am now in a church that gives high priority to worship and makes it a highlight of the week for church members.

I like the way Eddie Gibbs describes true worship: "The worship of God's people lifts us above the multitude of mundane concerns which surround us in our daily lives. It restores true perspective and challenges us to reorder our priorities as we dwell corporately in God's presence and see the world from His vantage point. Churches which are attracting significant numbers of those who were formerly nominal Christians are characterized by worship which expresses a transcendent dimension."[9]

Meaningful worship does not happen automatically—at least in our contemporary American culture. It has to be developed. Christian people need to be taught to worship. Whether the worship is contemporary or traditional, the service needs to be well organized if it is to bring God and His people together in a special way. I am convinced that many pastors and church leaders do not know enough about worship, nor do many of them realize its importance. When this is the case, a poor worship atmosphere can be a contributing factor to arrested spiritual development and an obstacle to church growth.

Willimon and Wilson say, "When a family moves to a new town and begins to look for a church, their first encounter with a church will, in the great majority of cases, be the Sunday morning worship service. If they like what they see and hear, if something seems to be happening there, they may return next week."[10] Some contemporary churches have gone so far as to design their entire worship experience as "seeker sensitive" so that it is geared to meet the expectations of the unchurched rather than those of believers. To avoid arrested spiritual development, seeker-sensitive churches conduct special teaching services specifically for believers at other times during the week.

VISION FOR THE WORLD

Something special happens in the Christian life when a person sees himself or herself living, praying and ministering in the context of what God is doing in the whole world. Isolation and

---

Churches are not meant to be centripetal, but centrifugal.

---

introversion occur when church members fail to stretch their vision past their own stained-glass windows. Not only knowing what God is doing in the world, but also participating in it in one way or another brings Christian maturity.

Churches that have developed strong and creative outreach and missionary programs have an advantage over those that have not. Recruiting young people for foreign service, whether for short-term or long-term service, and then receiving their reports, contribute substantially to a church's health. Generous giving for evangelistic work and for physical, social and material humanitarian needs also builds Christian vitality. Churches are not meant to be centripetal, but centrifugal. A significant part of their ministries needs to be directed toward others if churches are to be healthy.

Introverted and self-seeking Christians are likely to have arrested spiritual development. Building a missionary vision, a concern for the world and an excitement of sharing with others helps cure it.

TREATMENT FOR ARRESTED SPIRITUAL DEVELOPMENT

The approach to treating churches suffering from arrested spiritual development is twofold.

1. E-0 evangelism. If church members are not committed to Christ or converted or born again, reversing this situation is not just an option, it is a *necessity* if arrested spiritual development is ever going to be healed. For those seeking help with this process, I recommend Rob Smith's book *Leading Christians to Christ: Evangelizing the Church.* Perhaps one of Rob Smith's most important credentials is that he is an Episcopal priest. The Episcopal church is among those denominations that face a larger than average challenge for E-0 evangelism. Whether or not you are an Episcopalian, Smith's book will give you a rationale and some encouragement to help "the apparently barely conscious worshiper who seems to be fulfilling some vaguely perceived obligation to be [in church]."[11]

2. Church renewal. Almost all denominations have within them pockets of individuals who specialize in church renewal. Most of them are grossly underutilized, but they can often bring practical remedies for arrested spiritual development and do it without violating the traditions of the particular church.

Church renewal is not a cure-all for any disease a church might have. In many cases, however, it will help a church get back to the basics and open doors for more normal spiritual growth and development. Churches that are renewed can manage the other church illnesses much easier and more productively.

Notes

1. Eddie Gibbs, *In Name Only* (Wheaton, Ill.: BridgePoint Books, 1994), pp. 78-79.
2. "Ten Characteristics of a Healthy Church" and a diagnostic tool for evaluation are available from The Evangelistic Association of New England, 279 Cambridge Street, Burlington, MA 01803.
3. Lyle E. Schaller, *Assimilating New Members* (Nashville: Abingdon Press, 1978), p. 53.

4. Dean M. Kelley, *Why Conservative Churches Are Growing* (New York: HarperCollins Publishers, 1972), p. 86.
5. Thomas C. Oden, *Requiem: A Lament in Three Movements* (Nashville: Abingdon Press, 1995), p. 44.
6. Ibid., p. 47.
7. C. Peter Wagner's resources for discovering spiritual gifts, *Your Spiritual Gifts Can Help Your Church Grow*, the reproducible group study guide that accompanies it and the personal questionnaire, *Finding Your Spiritual Gifts*, are available from your local Christian bookstore or from Gospel Light Publications, 1-800-4-GOSPEL.
8. William H. Willimon and Robert L. Wilson, *Rekindling the Flame* (Nashville: Abingdon Press, 1987), p. 41.
9. Gibbs, *In Name Only*, p. 119.
10. Willimon and Wilson, *Rekindling the Flame*, p. 112.
11. Rob Smith, *Leading Christians to Christ: Evangelizing the Church* (Harrisburg, Pa.: Morehouse Publishing, 1990), p. xiii.

Chapter 9

ST. JOHN'S SYNDROME: WHY DOES A HOT CHURCH BECOME LUKEWARM?

St. John's Syndrome, like many human diseases, is named for the person who first discovered and described it. Hodgkin's Disease, for example, was named for Thomas Hodgkin; Parkinson's Disease was named for James Parkinson; and St. John's Syndrome is named for the apostle St. John. Although John didn't use the name, he described the disease in the well-known passage containing the letters to the seven churches of Asia Minor, in the book of Revelation, chapters two and three.

The underlying problem of St. John's Syndrome is Christian nominality. When Christians become Christians in name only, when they feel that their faith is only routine, when church involvement is largely going through the motions, and when belonging to church is nothing more than a family tradition and a social nicety, St. John's Syndrome is likely at work.

CHURCH LIFE CYCLES

Churches, like people, tend to go through life cycles, although there is a difference. The human life cycle is inevitable. There is no such thing as a fountain of youth. The church life cycle, however, is not inevitable. Decline, weakness and death can be avoided if St. John's Syndrome is understood, and if appropriate steps are taken to prevent it, as well as other known church diseases.

David Moberg, one of America's foremost sociologists of religion, describes the church life cycle in five stages: (1) the incipient organization, (2) the formal organization, (3) the stage of maximum efficiency, (4) the institutional stage and (5) disintegration.[1] St. John's Syndrome sets in during the institutional stage.

The phenomenon of St. John's Syndrome can be pictured by drawing a bell-shaped curve on a piece of graph paper. If the vertical axis of the graph is church membership, and the horizontal axis goes across time, the typical pattern will look something like a bell. The usual configuration is as follows: (1) *Rapid growth*. This is the upward curve on the left-hand side of the bell; (2) *Plateau*. This is when the curve begins to form the top of the bell; (3) *Decline*. This is the right-hand side of the bell on its downward curve; (4) *Stagnation*. Finally the curve flattens out at a low membership figure, and the church learns simply how to survive. After that, another disease such as ethnikitis might set in and finish off the church, or it might continue to limp along for a generation or two.

Although the time required for this to occur may vary from case to case, a common pattern is for the rapid-growth period to last about 20 years, the plateau for the next 10 years, and the decline from the thirtieth year onward. That is why I mentioned that the apostle John, writing about 40 years after the churches in Asia Minor were first planted, was more or less on the predictable time schedule.

These time sequences are not just an educated guess. They seemed to be confirmed by an interesting study conducted by Douglas Walrath about Reformed Church in America churches in the Albany, New York, area. Walrath developed a typology of churches and conducted what is called a "quadratic regression study" about the churches of each type. Many of his graphs look precisely like the St. John's Syndrome bell curve we have been describing. Unfortunately, this research has never been published, but I can report that it does give us some empirical indication that church leaders need to be aware of if they intend their churches to maintain satisfactory growth rates.

Arrested spiritual development and St. John's Syndrome have some common symptoms, so it is helpful to distinguish

---

St. John's Syndrome has a sociological explanation, being a disease that typically sets in with the second generation of Christians.

---

clearly between the two. Arrested spiritual development is a malady of this present generation of believers, brought on by certain choices they and their leaders have made. As individuals and as groups they consequently fail to develop spiritually as they should. St. John's Syndrome, on the other hand, has more of a *sociological* explanation, being a disease that typically sets in with the second generation of Christians.

LUKEWARM CHURCHES

Forty years was just about the length of time needed for the decline to set in among the first-century churches in Asia Minor. Their beginning is described in Acts 19. Paul was then on his third term as a missionary, and he stayed in the Ephesus area longer than he had stayed at any other place. People not only in the city of Ephesus, but also throughout the surrounding province of Asia Minor, were open to the preaching of Jesus Christ, and a considerable number of churches were started.

It was an exciting time. The churches were in their first stages of rapid growth. Public debates were being held. Synagogues split. Evil spirits were being cast out. Believers were speaking with tongues and prophesying. People were being healed of their diseases. Animists were finding Christ and burning their books and fetishes; one pile was said to be worth 50,000 pieces of silver or about $4 million in today's economy. The cult of Diana of the Ephesians was taking a beating. The city was in an uproar. Because their business had gone into a nosedive, the pagan silversmiths rioted. Few would buy the idols they had been manufacturing.

Ephesus became the center of evangelistic work for the whole district. From there, Paul trained church planters in the school of Tyrannus, and sent them round about until "all who dwelt in Asia heard the word of the Lord Jesus, both Jews and Greeks" (Acts 19:10). It was the greatest evangelistic harvest the apostle Paul had ever experienced or would ever experience in the future.

Forty years later, however, the church was in a different condition. St. John's Syndrome had set in. To read John's account of the church at Ephesus in Revelation is saddening. Nothing is said there about power encounters, animists burning fetishes, people being healed, silversmiths rioting or new converts being added to the church daily. The flames of evangelism apparently had died down to a flicker, and the church was said to have left its "first love" (Rev. 2:4).

What had happened? It had become a second-generation church. The cost of becoming a Christian was minimal for those who had been born and raised in Christian families. Back when their parents had first become Christians they were threatened and persecuted. The cost of discipleship was high, and they had paid the price. When their children became believers it was vastly different. They received a smile and a pat on the back rather than insults and beatings. They were neither cold nor hot, but lukewarm (see 3:15,16).

FAITH FROM TRADITION, NOT FROM EXPERIENCE

Eddie Gibbs says it well. In what I consider the best book available about the causes and cure of St. John's Syndrome (although Gibbs does not use that phrase), *In Name Only*, Gibbs says, "The nominality problem is accentuated when the second generation becomes the dominant group. Unlike the pioneers, who experienced the alienation, hardships and deliverances, the second generation has been nurtured all along within the religious community. This second generation learns of God's mighty acts through receiving the tradition rather than from firsthand experience."[2]

In the letters to all seven churches in Asia Minor, several particular symptoms are mentioned. The "doctrine of Balaam" (2:14), for example, may have been a reduction of strictness in the church through intermarriage with the heathen people. Although the intermarriage problem may be more acute in some situations than in others, the need to maintain strictness is important for a religious organization that wants to grow. Dean Kelley has shown this in his book *Why Conservative Churches Are Growing*, which I mentioned in the last chapter.

Another example is the "doctrine of the Nicolaitans" (v. 15). This may have meant the imposition of the rule of the clergy over the laity in the church, because the root words are *nikao*, which means "to conquer," and *laos*, which means "the people." If it does signify clericalism, this is well known to be a widespread problem among churches today that have St. John's Syndrome.

In chapter one, I explained that one of the fundamental axioms of church growth is that the people must want their church to grow and be willing to pay the price. They must be ready and willing to commit themselves—their time, energy and money—to growth. They should be discovering, developing and using their spiritual gifts. Pastors who think they should be doing virtually all the ministry of the church themselves, and not delegate it to the laypeople, usually do not stimulate solid growth dynamics. They can be seen as present-day Nicolaitans.

REDEMPTION AND LIFT

Although it is not necessary here to continue to list in detail the problems of the churches in first-century Asia Minor, one more should be mentioned because it is frequently associated with St. John's Syndrome. This is affluence produced by what missiologists call "redemption and lift." The church at Laodicea was characterized as rich and comfortable, but spiritually poor (see v. 17).

As a general rule, the gospel takes root in a new culture or people group among the simple, working-class people as opposed to the rich and powerful elite. A good example of this is the ministry of John Wesley. As Willimon and Wilson remind us, "John Wesley felt a strong mandate to reach the mass of people who were unchurched and had not responded to the gospel....For the most part he did not seek out or attempt to evangelize the upper classes. No Methodist preaching post was established in any of the five most privileged boroughs of London. The poor heard him gladly."[3]

Poorer people, through their new commitment to Christ, frequently develop upward social mobility. In a generation or so, they are not usually as poor as they used to be, and some have also become well-off. In such a situation, they can find themselves cut off socially from their own non-Christian friends and relatives who are still poor. This goes along with St. John's Syndrome in many cases. Although nothing is intrinsically wrong with honestly acquired affluence, if upward mobility cuts off Christians from the further opportunity of winning lost people from their own social group to Christ, it can halt growth.

In extreme cases, such as the one described in James 2, people in upward mobility can sometimes *despise* their former peers. James said, "If there should come into your assembly a man with gold rings, in fine apparel, and there should also come in a poor man in filthy clothes, and you pay attention to the one wearing the fine clothes...have you not shown partiality among yourselves, and become judges with evil thoughts?" (Jas. 2:2-4). It needs to be understood that affluence, in certain circumstances, can be a growth problem for churches. The solution is not to make poverty a virtue, but to manage affluence with the fruit of the Spirit.

Within 40 years, at least one of the churches in Asia Minor, once very much alive spiritually, was considered dead, and others were not far from it (see Rev. 3:1). They were still surviving as social institutions, but because of St. John's Syndrome, the vitality of the first generation of Christians had been sapped away, and therefore the churches had become a disappointment to God.

LEAVING THE FIRST LOVE

St. John writes in Revelation 2:4 that Jesus had something

against the church in Ephesus because it "left its first love."
I have heard several preachers attach a variety of meanings
to leaving the first love. The Scriptures do not tell us definitely
what the first love of the church at Ephesus might have been.
Some interpret it as human love, some interpret it as love for
God. It seems more likely to me, however, that it would refer
to love for lost men and women in need of reconciliation to
God. If the church at Ephesus was anything in its first generation, it was a center of aggressive evangelism. Paul stayed there
for three years (see Acts 20:31) and Ephesus became his second
primary base for missionary work, Antioch being the first (see
13:1-3; 14:26; 15:40; 18:23). His intention after the three years in
Ephesus was to move his base to Rome, and for that reason he
wrote the Epistle to the Romans right after his ministry in
Ephesus (see Rom. 15:23,24). The church at Ephesus was the
mother church of all the other churches in Asia Minor. It was
growing both by expansion and by extension.

Such an expression of love and concern for those who are
not saved is a common characteristic of a new church, still in
its early stage of rapid growth. The healthy growth line is the
left side of the bell curve I described earlier. At that stage, the
church perceives itself as existing primarily for others, not for
itself. Consequently, the blessing of God comes and the church
grows. Evangelism is the top outreach priority of such a
church, as it was in Ephesus.

A growth problem is bound to arise when the outreach priorities of the church are switched. This has nothing to do with
other kinds of priorities, such as bringing unbelievers to a
commitment to Christ and a commitment to the Body of
Christ, both of which I believe need to precede outreach. If a
church that is otherwise in good health, however, allows nominality to dim its belief that people without God have no hope,
either in this world or in the world to come, and if the church
does not act on this belief with forthright evangelism, St.
John's Syndrome will have taken its toll.

Evangelism, of course, is only one facet of the totality of
God's mission in the world. The cultural mandate stands tall
alongside the evangelistic mandate. Jesus told us to love our
neighbor as ourselves (see Matt. 22:39). Christian social concerns need to be, and are, widely expressed in the world. Jesus
said: "The Spirit of the Lord is upon Me, because He has

anointed Me to preach the gospel to the poor. He has sent Me to heal the brokenhearted, to proclaim liberty to the captives, and recovery of sight to the blind" (Luke 4:18) The cultural mandate is not optional for biblical Christians.

The evangelistic mandate, however, looks at human beings in a slightly different way. It does not see people so much as naked or clothed, hungry or full, oppressed or liberated. It sees people rather as lost or saved, condemned or justified, estranged or reconciled, on the way to heaven or on the way to hell. Both ways of looking at people are correct and together they reflect God's own perspective.

THE PRIORITY OF EVANGELISM

Although both evangelism and social concern are vital parts of the mission of the church in the world, evangelism should be regarded as the top priority. As the Lausanne Covenant affirms, "In the church's mission of sacrificial service evangelism is primary." I fully realize that some will read this and disagree. They feel that the two emphases ought to be equal, or even that social concern should be supreme. Their Christian compassion is commendable, but they should realize they are suggesting a formula that predictably will cause churches to plateau and decline.

Some of the old-line churches in America have discovered this recently. During the past 50 years, 1946 to 1996, the seven largest predominantly Anglo denominations (United Methodist Church, Evangelical Lutheran Church in America, the Presbyterian Church [U.S.A.], the Lutheran Church-Missouri Synod, the Episcopal Church, the United Church of Christ and the American Baptist Churches in the U.S.A., including their predecessors) lost two-thirds of their constituency.[*]

Special task forces have been named by these denominations to try to uncover the problems that have caused the decline. The reports that have been written conclude first of all that church growth is complex. In no case can one simplistic, generalized reason explain why churches grow or decline. As I understand the reports, however, they do confirm that taking strong stands for social concern, to the detriment of carrying out the evangelistic mandate, has been one of the major causes of church decline in America.

THE TURMOIL OF THE SIXTIES

It is easy to see why church decline could have occurred in the 1960s. The Vietnam War, the civil rights movement, the development of a hippie counterculture, the death-of-God movement—all combined to stir the nation to its core. American society was in a turmoil. Church bureaucrats, like other Americans, felt these problems deeply, and they used their influence to do what they felt was necessary to heal society. In the process, they initiated a profound change in ministry priorities that eventually affected their churches at the grassroots. They quickly entered into the most severe church membership decline in American history.

Sociological studies have shown that members left mainline churches that had been taking strong social positions, not because the churches became socially involved, but because in doing so, the churches had relegated evangelism to a secondary position. In one of the studies commissioned by the National Council of Churches, Douglas Johnson and George Cornell said: "Summing up, America's churches are chiefly dedicated to that old-time endeavor that never gets old, spreading the Gospel....Whether they see it in terms of prayer or evangelism, however, it is considered the local church's central imperative by Christians across the continent, black and white, city folks and back countrymen."[5]

If those occupying the power positions in the denominations would have heeded the report filed by Johnson and Cornell back in the early '70s and acted on it, the shape of American Christianity might be different today. They could have taken steps to cure St. John's Syndrome in its early stages, but they did not. They instead continued to highlight theological and ethical reasons why social activism should take priority over soul-winning evangelism.

The denominational leaders attempted to explain their losses as being caused by *contextual* factors (over which they would have had no control) as opposed to *institutional* factors (which would have included their own tragic decisions about switching priorities). The net result was that, looking at the social arena alone, they ironically were *losing* social influence in America. The National Council of Churches is today a mere shadow of what it was four decades ago before its denominational leaders decided to give evangelism a lower priority.

WHAT IS THE MEANING OF LIFE?

When the average Christian, or non-Christian, for that matter, perceives that a church is giving evangelism anything other than top priority in its outreach ministry, the church is perceived to be weak and unattractive. Dean Kelley anticipated this early in the decline. He said, "If a religion should set out deliberately to benefit the whole society by patriotic preaching

---

The Gallup poll found that 42 percent of America's evangelicals are involved in helping the poor, the sick, the handicapped and the elderly, compared to only 26 percent of the nonevangelical Christians.

---

or welfare services or social action, but *did not make life meaningful for its members*, it would benefit the whole society less than if it had contented itself with ministering its unique function to those who looked to it for that ministry" (emphasis his).[6]

Average citizens may be interested in helping less fortunate neighbors as much as possible, but they are clearly a good deal more interested in comprehending the ultimate meaning of life. Many social institutions can offer help to the poor and oppressed, but only the churches can answer the question in the minds of almost all humans: When I die am I going to heaven or to hell? That is an ultimate issue and Christianity can provide a clear answer. Churches that wish to avoid the decline represented by the right-hand side of St. John's Syndrome bell curve need to be prepared to provide the biblical answer to that question at all times and keep this function as their highest priority for ministry.

Churches might be surprised to find that when they give

evangelism first priority, the result is more and better social work. The Gallup poll tested this at one point by comparing the social involvement of evangelical churches, which typically give the evangelistic mandate first priority, to that of other churches, which are more likely to treat evangelism as secondary. They found that 42 percent of America's evangelicals are involved in helping the poor, the sick, the handicapped and the elderly, compared to only 26 percent of the nonevangelical Christians.

PREVENTING
ST. JOHN'S SYNDROME

The best approach to St. John's Syndrome is preventive, rather than therapeutic, medicine. It is much easier to avoid it than to recover from it. Recovering from it might require a cure similar to that of ethnikitis—a complete blood transfusion. That in itself should probably be seen not so much as curing the disease, but rather as a way of dying with dignity.

SECRETS OF THE SOUTHERN
BAPTIST GROWTH

Notably, what is now the largest Protestant denomination in America—the Southern Baptist Convention—was continually gaining members during the last three decades while the other formerly mainline denominations were decreasing. The three chief reasons for this were all institutional factors, because contextual factors were the same for Southern Baptists and others that were gaining members as they were for the denominations that were losing.

For one thing, the Southern Baptists kept evangelism as their number one priority. The fierce internal struggles between Southern Baptist conservatives and liberals that received much publicity during the 1980s was essentially about this issue. If the liberals instead of the conservatives had come out on top, it would not have been surprising to have seen the Southern Baptists going the route of the United Methodists, the Presbyterian Church (U.S.A.) and others.

For another thing, Southern Baptists never contracted the disease of people-blindness. Under the creative leadership of

Oscar Romo of their Home Mission Board, they vigorously followed the strategy of multiplying churches specific to each one of the people groups in the United States rather than insisting that those of varying cultures worship together in the same local congregation. As a result, Southern Baptists have become,

---

"Unless countermeasures are taken, the strength of a new religion tends to weaken from one generation to the next....There tends to be a lukewarmness in the children of believers and their children."

---

by far, the most multiethnic denomination in the country.

The third reason Southern Baptists have continued to grow and avoided St. John's Syndrome pertains to the Sunday School as a central part of their denominational philosophy of ministry. Studies of the denominations that have been losing members have shown that one factor across the board has been their inability to persuade their children to join their parents' churches. A study of United Methodist churches showed that 21.3 percent of church members were age 65 and over, compared with 11.5 percent of the total population. On the other end of the scale, Methodists had only 12.4 percent of members in the 19- to 34-year-old group, while the nation had 28.4 percent.[7]

One of the strongest arguments for the Sunday School as a key for preventing St. John's Syndrome comes from Southern Baptist church growth expert, Thom Rainer, in his excellent book *Giant Awakenings*. He begins with a quote from Dean Hoge, Benton Johnson and Donald A. Luidens: "But unless countermeasures are taken, the strength of a new religion tends to weaken from one generation to the next....There tends to be a lukewarmness in the children of believers and *their chil-*

dren."[8] A more concise statement describing St. John's Syndrome could hardly be made.

Thom Rainer goes on to argue that the principal function of the Sunday School is not so much entertaining kids with Bible stories or providing warm fellowship groups for adults, although these functions are important. He stresses that the essence of Sunday School, as Southern Baptists have traditionally understood it, "is a method of teaching, with conviction and depth, the whole counsel of biblical truths to all ages," and he goes on to say, "A true Sunday School must see as its ongoing purpose the communication and teaching of the faith to all generations."[9]

Some may say, "But a strong Sunday School is not part of our tradition." This may be true, but if it is not, some functional substitute must be found if nominality and St. John's Syndrome is to be prevented.

AN INFLOW OF FIRST-GENERATION CHRISTIANS

There is another sure-fire prevention of St. John's Syndrome. Because it is largely a disease of second-generation Christians, it can be prevented by making certain that a large number of *first-generation* Christians always attend the church. Like koinonitis, St. John's Syndrome can be prevented or cured by steady conversion growth. Biological growth alone will tend to encourage St. John's Syndrome. Transfer growth may or may not help, depending on the kind of people who are transferring into the church. If the people transferring in are nominal Christians, it will not likely help. An influx of new Christians, however, freshly converted babes in Christ, who will soon grow and mature and reproduce themselves, will keep the church healthy, vigorous and growing, as long as the supply lasts.

Restoring the first love can turn a lukewarm church once again into a hot church!

Notes

1. David O. Moberg, *The Church as a Social Institution* (Upper Saddle River, N.J.: Prentice Hall, 1962), pp. 118-123.
2. Eddie Gibbs, *In Name Only* (Wheaton, Ill.: BridgePoint Books, 1994), pp. 43-44.
3. William H. Willimon and Robert L. Wilson, *Rekindling the Flame* (Nashville: Abingdon Press, 1987), p. 39.
4. Lyle E. Schaller, *The New Reformation: Tomorrow Arrived Yesterday* (Nashville: Abingdon Press, 1995), p. 48.
5. Douglas W. Johnson and George W. Cornell, *Punctured Preconceptions* (New York: Friendship Press, 1972), p. 108.
6. Dean M. Kelley, *Why Conservative Churches Are Growing* (New York: HarperCollins Publishers, 1972), p. 45.
7. Willimon and Wilson, *Rekindling the Flame*, p. 18.
8. Thom S. Rainer, *Giant Awakenings* (Nashville: Broadman & Holman Publishers, 1995), p. 49.
9. Ibid, p. 53.

Chapter 10

HYPOPNEUMIA: COME, HOLY SPIRIT!

*hypopneumia (hi´-po-noo´-me-a), n. subnormal min-
istry of the Holy Spirit in a Christian individual, a
church, or other Christian group. [< Gk, hypó, below;
pneuma, wind; spirit].*

As I have indicated several times, the factors affecting the
growth or nongrowth of churches can be grouped under three
headings: contextual factors, institutional factors and spiritual
factors.

By way of review, the two terminal illnesses of churches,
ethnikitis and ghost town disease, are primarily caused by
contextual factors, sociological conditions of which the church
and its leaders have no control. People-blindness, hyper-cooperativism, koinonitis and sociological strangulation are primarily caused by *institutional* factors of which church leaders
do have considerable control. Arrested spiritual development
and St. John's syndrome are also rooted in institutional factors, but spiritual factors emerge as well.

Hypopneumia, more than any of the other diseases, is rooted in *spiritual* factors. It would be important to clarify at this

point that the three categories are not mutually exclusive. To one degree or another, all three, contextual, institutional and spiritual, can play a role in any of the diseases, depending on circumstances. Some might argue, for example, that koinonitis has spiritual dimensions or that people-blindness can be influenced by contextual factors.

When I completed my initial research and compiled my first list of church diseases, I had not as yet developed a sensitivity to spiritual factors. None of the leaders professionally identifying with the Church Growth Movement at that time were highlighting the diseases. This is not to say that any of us *disbelieved* in the power of the Holy Spirit or in prayer or in spiritual warfare, but rather than surfacing these things as potentially crucial growth factors, we simply *assumed* them and said little about them.

SURFACING THE SPIRITUAL FACTORS

The assumption about spiritual factors has since changed, largely because some of our critics began to bring it to our attention and to the attention of the general public through their writings. The late Herbert Kane, for example, wrote a commendatory chapter about the Church Growth Movement, but then added at the conclusion: "The proponents of church growth, with few exceptions, have emphasized the human factors and all but overlooked the divine factor."[1] When I first read this, my immediate reaction, I must admit, was a bit defensive. Then I realized, however, that if I were to be honest, I would admit that I was in denial and that Kane was right. So from then on I began dedicating a good deal of my research time to spiritual factors.

My first project was to look into the relationship of supernatural signs and wonders to the growth of churches. John Wimber helped my understanding in that area more than anyone else. My book *How to Have a Healing Ministry in Any Church* (Regal Books), summarizes that research.

I then began an intensive study of prayer and wrote the "Prayer Warrior Series": *Warfare Prayer, Prayer Shield, Breaking Strongholds in Your City, Churches That Pray* and *Confronting the Powers* (Regal Books). When these books were first released, some observers remarked, "Peter Wagner is now moving away from church growth and getting into prayer." This was not my intention at all. I do not see prayer and church growth as two separate categories. Rather, I see prayer and other spiritual factors as much a part of church growth as the pastoral leadership or the small groups or the location of the church or the size of the parking lot or any other recognized factor affecting the growth or decline of churches.

THE HUNGER FOR GOD'S SPIRIT

More recently, some of the younger church growth authors have begun giving spiritual factors a high-profile position in their analyses of growth and nongrowth. For example, a prominent church researcher, George Barna, did an extensive study of what he calls "user friendly churches"—churches that are attracting and keeping newcomers on a sustained basis.

Barna reports: "Prayer was one of the foundation stones of ministry in the user friendly churches examined...People in these churches were more likely than usual to view prayer as an opportunity to be in the presence of God, and to be filled with His mind. They were more likely than usual to insist that prayer be a central part of any decisions made by the church."[2]

Thom Rainer is the dean of the Billy Graham School of Missions, Evangelism, and Church Growth in The Southern Baptist Theological Seminary, and a prolific writer in the field of church growth. Rainer is convinced that traditional churches, many of which have become ill and stagnated, can be awakened and can see new life flow through them. He perceives nine current trends that can greatly help traditional churches.

The first chapter of Rainer's book about the subject, *Giant Awakenings*, focuses on the great prayer movement. He begins by saying, "If church futurists are indeed overlooking some of the spiritual aspects of the twenty-first-century church, we must discern where the most glaring omissions occur. With only a few exceptions, the pundits fail to see the immeasurable impact that prayer has upon the churches."[3]

Thom Rainer has found that "members of traditional churches are hungry for a great touch of God's Spirit."[4] Although he doesn't use the word, Rainer senses that many churches realize they are suffering from hypopneumia and that they are actively looking for a cure.

Glen Martin and Gary McIntosh say, "The goal should be to have prayer as foundational to all church ministries. Prayer should be a significant, rather than a cosmetic agenda item. It should become a natural thing for people to pray about everything—decisions, problems, giving thanks for good things, praying for each other, asking God's blessing and guidance before each ministry activity."[5]

WHAT IS HYPOPNEUMIA?

The name "hypopneumia" is new, but very precise. It is a church disease caused by a subnormal level of the presence and power of the Holy Spirit in the life and ministry of the church. In medical terminology, "hypo" means too little of something, and "hyper" means too much. For example, many are familiar with the terms "hypothyroidism" and "hyperthyroidism," indicating deficient activity of the thyroid gland as opposed to excessive activity of the thyroid gland. Other terms are "hypothermia," subnormal body temperature, and "hyperthermia," a fever.

The biblical word *pneuma* is the word for Spirit, as in Holy Spirit. Many might recognize that medical science uses the same Greek word for pneumonia, a disease affecting the lungs or the "breath" of an individual. I am not sure that a church could have a disease of "hyperpneumia," or too much of the Holy Spirit, although I am conscious of the fact that some believers of a more traditional bent might think that some contemporary renewal groups suffer from such a malady. I am quite sure, however, that too many churches are not growing because of "hypopneumia," too little of the Holy Spirit.

SYMPTOMS OF HYPOPNEUMIA

The symptoms of hypopneumia are a bit more elusive than those of some of the other church diseases. An entry level church consultant could rapidly diagnose ethnikitis or sociological strangulation or koinonitis in most cases. Likewise, a medical doctor can readily diagnose most cases of hypertension or measles or a stroke, but the diagnosis of other things such as chronic fatigue syndrome or certain allergies or a nutritional deficiency is often more elusive.

I believe it is fair to assume that the Holy Spirit is present in every church, just as vitamins are present in every human body. The question then becomes: Is there enough? Enough for what? In answer to that, let me say that I continually try to keep enough Vitamin C in my body to prevent colds, and years can and do go by without my catching a cold. At the same time, I realize that many in the health care field scoff at the idea that colds can be prevented by using Vitamin C. They might suggest that I have a natural immunity to colds that would be in operation whether or not I used a daily Vitamin C supplement, and that I would be acquiring all the Vitamin C I need in my regular diet. This is a familiar example from the medical field.

In churches, the presence of the Holy Spirit is similar. Pastors and other leaders frequently debate with each other about how much the Holy Spirit should be emphasized, and what kinds of manifestations of the Holy Spirit should be welcomed in churches. It is often hard to know where to draw the line, but saying this is not to deny that a line can and does exist. Some churches could be described as spiritually dead. The church continues to exist, but the power of God is notably absent. This would be a church suffering from hypopneumia.

Ron Crandall, an Asbury Theological Seminary professor, has done a careful study of strategies that have caused small, stagnant churches to turn around and begin to grow. One of the chapters in his book *Turnaround Strategies for the Small Church*, is titled "Turning Toward the Spirit." He says, "It is not a new problem for the people of God to turn away from the Spirit and ignore the counsel of God."[6] This is another way of saying that some churches suffer from hypopneumia. Crandall goes on to say that the symptoms seen in such churches revolve around helplessness and hopelessness.

THE CHANGE MUST BE SUPERNATURAL

What can be done for churches that are experiencing a run-down condition because of a subnormal level of spiritual power? Ron Crandall has seen pastors who have brought new courage, empowerment and imagination to these kinds of sick churches. How? He says, "The change must be supernatural. Turnaround pastors are quick to affirm that they do not produce this change; rather, they lead their congregations into the presence of the risen Christ and pray and wait for the Holy

---

My prescriptions for a cure to hypopneumia are broader than specific signs of the manifestation of the Holy Spirit....churches suffering from hypopneumia need more of (1) the fruit of the Holy Spirit and (2) the power of the Holy Spirit.

Spirit once more to transform struggling and defeated disciples into men and women of radiant hope."[7]

I love that phrase: *pray and wait for the Holy Spirit.* The cure for hypopneumia is so obvious that it almost goes without saying. If our church has too *little* of the Holy Spirit, the cure is to acquire *more* of the Holy Spirit. Things will clearly go better when more of the Holy Spirit is present. Even if you believe your church might have only a mild case of hypopneumia, acquiring more of the Holy Spirit might be good advice.

At this point, I expect that many church leaders are wondering where I am planning to take them. Most of us have received our spiritual formation in certain church traditions, the boundaries of which are, in part, described by specific beliefs concerning the Holy Spirit. Some might say they want more of the Holy Spirit, but they don't want to be Pentecostals or they don't want to fall down on the floor or they don't want to give up their hymnals or they don't want to speak in tongues or they don't want people shouting in their services. I fully understand such concerns, and I think none of those things are necessarily cures for hypopneumia, but I also think any of them could be a legitimate way for the

Holy Spirit to show His presence on certain occasions.

My prescriptions for a cure to hypopneumia are broader than specific signs of the manifestation of the Holy Spirit. I would argue that churches suffering from hypopneumia need more of (1) the *fruit* of the Holy Spirit and (2) the *power* of the Holy Spirit.

IS IT RIGHT TO
STRESS THE HOLY SPIRIT?

Some Church traditions tend to reduce the teaching about the Holy Spirit or mentioning the Holy Spirit to a minimum. They believe that Christians today should focus on the second Person of the Trinity much more than on the third Person of the Trinity. This attitude, I am afraid, has been one of the major contributors to hypopneumia.

If you suspect that your church might be suffering from hypopneumia, my advice is to start responding to it by realizing how important the third Person of the Trinity is supposed to be in our daily lives as Christians. We need to overcome our inhibitions, get out of long-standing denial and affirm the ministry of the Holy Spirit clearly and specifically. An excellent way to do this, I have found, is to return to what Jesus, the second Person of the Trinity, said about the matter.

THE HOLY SPIRIT IS AN
ADVANTAGE

Jesus' disciples had been with Him personally for a year and a half. They had grown to love Him, they had committed their lives to His cause, and they could think of nothing better in life than to travel with and eat with and minister with the Son of God, the second Person of the Trinity. They may have had some trials and tribulations, but deep down they were happy and content.

Their contentment was shattered one day when Jesus made an announcement to them: He was preparing to leave! This shocking news produced confusion, disbelief and a protest, verbalized mostly by Peter, who argued strongly with the Master. It became so heated that Jesus said, "Get behind me, Satan!" The disciples were so stunned that it took them some time to realize that what Jesus had told them was true, and that the time would soon come when He no longer would be there with them.

After things cooled down, Jesus began to explain the details of what He had in mind for the future. This is related mostly in John 14 and 16. Jesus acknowledged to them, "Because I have said these things to you, sorrow has filled your heart"

Jesus told His disciples that they would be <u>better</u> <u>off</u> with the immediate presence of the third Person of the Trinity than they had been with the presence of the second Person of the Trinity.

(John 16:6). This He followed by an extremely important state-ment: "Nevertheless I tell you the truth. It is to your advantage that I go away." To the disciples' *advantage* that the second Person of the Trinity leave them? How could anyone be better off than being physically present with the Son of God? Jesus answered the question in their minds by saying, "For if I do not go away, the *Helper* will not come to you; but if I depart, I will send Him to you" (v. 7, emphasis mine).

Who, then, was this Helper? None other, of course, than the Holy Spirit, the third Person of the Trinity. As clearly and plainly as He had said anything, Jesus told His disciples that they would be *better off* with the immediate presence of the third Person of the Trinity than they had been with the pres-ence of the second Person of the Trinity. Such a notion is as hard for many of us today to assimilate as it was for the disci-ples in the first century. But it is true, and believing it is an important first step toward curing hypopneumia.

By the time Jesus left, His disciples had received the finest training any Christian worker could ask for. For three years, they sat at the feet of the Master. They learned about theology, ethics, evangelism, prayer, healing, spiritual warfare, casting out demons, morality, homiletics, stewardship and biblical interpretation from the greatest Teacher in history. Jesus was training them to be His principal agents for extending the kingdom of God when He left. That superb training, however, was not enough for the task ahead.

TARRYING IN JERUSALEM

Jesus told His disciples that when He went away, they should not go right out and try to put into practice what He had taught them. They were not to scatter and preach the gospel of the Kingdom immediately. Instead, Jesus said, "Tarry in the city of Jerusalem until you are endued with power from on high" (Luke 24:49). All their high-quality learning was not enough. The very last words Jesus spoke to conclude His three years here on earth were: "But you shall receive power when the Holy Spirit has come upon you; and you shall be witnesses to Me in Jerusalem, and in all Judea and Samaria, and to the end of the earth" (Acts 1:8). Immediately following that He was taken up to heaven in a cloud.

The disciples obeyed. They went to Jerusalem, entered an Upper Room and they "continued with one accord in prayer and supplication" (v. 14). Then came the Day of Pentecost, the Holy Spirit did endue them with power from on high and the net result is that Christianity has been spreading around the world in a remarkable fashion for two thousand years.

Most churches that have hypopneumia would agree that what I have just said is true. They agree because they believe the Bible, and this is obviously one thing the Bible says. But they do not seem to talk about this much. They do not highlight the person and work of the Holy Spirit nearly as much as they highlight the Father and the Son. Some of them argue that it is wrong to talk a lot about the Holy Spirit, and sometimes they apologize when they find themselves doing it, for fear that they might be offending Jesus.

This is the main reason I have taken so much space to remind us exactly what Jesus' attitude was to our need for the person and the ministry of the Holy Spirit on an ongoing basis. Nothing is wrong with featuring the third Person of the Trinity in our church life because Jesus told us it would be to our advantage to do so.

None of this is to say that we should talk about, honor and worship the Father and the Son any less than we do. We do not cure hypopneumia by *subtracting*, but by *adding*. There should be no question that we are supposed to exalt Father,

---

Some churches focus on the Father and the Son, and the Spirit is often thought of as a "holy ghost" floating out there somewhere in the background. The price they can pay for this is hypopneumia.

Son and Holy Spirit—the three in One. The issue we face at the moment is that some churches do not do it. They focus on the Father and the Son, and the Spirit is often thought of as a "holy ghost" floating out there somewhere in the background. The price they can pay for this is hypopneumia.

BE FILLED WITH THE SPIRIT

The first step toward a cure for hypopneumia is to recognize the role the Holy Spirit is meant to have in our individual lives and in the lives of our churches and to be open to His ministry. The second step is to be filled with the Holy Spirit.

Is it possible to know whether or not you are filled with the Holy Spirit? Apparently, according to Scripture, it is just as possible as knowing whether you are drunk or not. At least Paul makes that comparison when he says, "Do not be drunk with wine, in which is dissipation; but be filled with the Spirit" (Eph. 5:18).

I think a "church" per se cannot be filled with the Holy Spirit over a sustained period of time. It is only as the individuals associated with the congregation are filled that corporately the church as an institution can be regarded as filled. There are exceptions to this rule, however. Many cases are on record in which the Holy Spirit, by a sovereign move of grace, has decided to visit a congregation in power. Some call this "spiritual awakening," some call it "renewal," some call it a "refreshing," some call it "revival." Whatever the name, the most immediate visible result is that individual lives are changed for the good, some quite dramatically. Dead churches have come alive almost overnight. Sometimes the change is short-lived, but other times it lasts for a generation or more.

Let's call it spiritual awakening. How does genuine spiritual awakening come to a church suffering from hypopneumia? For a long time, Christian leaders have debated with each other whether we can make certain decisions or we can do things to create conditions that open the way for the Holy Spirit to come to our churches with spiritual awakening. Some agree with Charles Finney that such preconditions do exist, but others move more toward the side of the sovereignty of God. In my opinion, it could well be "both-and" instead of "either-or." Sometimes God decides to move sovereignly and sometimes He moves in response to expressions of the heartfelt desire of His people.

THE PRECONDITION: A PRAYING CONGREGATION

If how God moves is true even to a degree, prayer is by consensus the principal precondition. Improving the prayer life of the church is one of those things that can be determined through the desires of the church members and their commitment to do whatever might be necessary to bring a spiritual awakening to the church. The change needs to take place on two fronts: (1) individuals and families, and (2) the corporate church life. No remedy for hypopneumia is more powerful than prayer. Obviously, individuals must agree to pray, desire to pray, and pray. The process, however, must move from number one to number two, and the church also must become a church of prayer.

In George Barna's study of turnaround churches—churches that once had suffered growth-obstructing diseases of one kind or another, but then recovered from them and subsequently grew—here is one of the interesting things he found: "It is not enough for the pastor to pray fervently, nor is it sufficient for a leadership team to pray ardently on behalf of the congregation. Until the church owns prayer as a world-class weapon in the battle against evil and cherishes prayer as a means of intimate and constant communication with God, the turnaround efforts of a body are severely limited, if not altogether doomed, to failure."[8]

One of the things for which the church should ask God, naturally, is a spiritual awakening. Prayer will be the chief force to move the congregation into a mode that responds correctly to Jesus' own plea to the church in Laodecia, a church that obviously was suffering from hypopneumia because it was "lukewarm, and neither cold nor hot" (Rev. 3:16). Jesus said to the believers in Laodecia: "Behold, I stand at the door and knock. If anyone hears My voice and opens the door, I will come in to him and dine with him, and he with Me" (v. 20). If our churches today open the door by praying for spiritual awakening, Jesus will come, not physically, but through the Holy Spirit.

THE PASTOR IS CRUCIAL

As I researched prayer in local churches for my book *Churches That Pray* (Regal Books), I found myself coming to a reluctant conclusion. I say "reluctant" because my counsel to pastors is always to delegate as much of the ministry of the church as possible to others and spend time training and encouraging the ministry of the laity. At first, I thought the prayer ministry of the church was one of those many areas of ministry that could be delegated, but I soon found I was wrong. By that I do not mean that the pastor cannot delegate the *administration* of the church's prayer ministry to others, but I do mean that the pastor must take personal *leadership* of the prayer life of the church.

The prayer ministry of a local church will rise or fall on the personal modeling of prayer in the life and activities of the senior pastor. To the degree that the pastor communicates to the congregation that prayer is a high priority item in personal life, in family life and in church life, the quality of prayer will rise. Except for a few exceptions, the water level of prayer, so to speak, will tend to rise as high as the pastor allows it to rise, and no higher.

This is not to say that without the leadership of the pastor churches will be prayerless. No, some prayer will almost always be present, but generally carried on by certain gifted intercessors and those in their immediate circles of influence. Without the overt support of the pastor, few churches have become fervent praying churches and taken this important step in curing hypopneumia.

ASKING FOR THE FILLING

Many of us might hesitate to use the expression "filled with the Holy Spirit" because we do not care to be directly identified with promoting certain anticipated outward manifestations of the Spirit seen in some circles. At the same time, we all are aware that the phrase is biblical and that God does desire to fill us with the Holy Spirit. Particularly those of us from traditions that would not self-identify as Pentecostal or charismatic need to come to terms with this dilemma better than we have in the past. If, for example, Paul instructs the believers in the church in Ephesus in general to be filled with the Holy Spirit (see Eph. 5:18), we should also expect God to fill us with the Holy Spirit no matter what our church tradition might be.

How can we receive that filling? I believe it is much less complicated than some might consider. It is not always necessary for us to get up and go forward during an emotional moment in the service or for someone to lay hands on us or to experience physical shaking or falling to the floor, although many are wonderfully filled with the Spirit through such experiences.

I do not believe I am oversimplifying the matter when I say that the most common way to be filled with the Holy Spirit is just to ask God to do it. Jesus said that if a son asks for bread, his father will not give him a stone or if he asks for an egg his father will not give him a scorpion. Likewise, He says, "How much more will your heavenly Father give the Holy Spirit to those who ask Him!" (Luke 11:13). This is nothing less than a divine promise!

Considering God's promise, I hope I am not seen as displaying spiritual arrogance to say that today I think I am, in fact, filled with the Holy Spirit. The reason I believe I am is that this morning I asked God specifically and directly to fill me with the Holy Spirit, and I have learned that God keeps His promises. I asked for "bread" and I don't think I got a stone. As a matter of fact, I make a habit to ask God for this *every* morning, day in and day out. The reason for this is that I have not come to a strong enough personal conclusion about how long the filling of the Holy Spirit lasts to take a chance.

Without wanting to push Paul's analogy too far, it is, however, a well-known fact that being drunk with wine lasts only for a day, and therefore we may be expected to renew our filling with the Holy Spirit daily. As I say, I am not absolutely sure such is the case, but because it is not that difficult to do, why not ask for a new filling every day?

The problem in many churches suffering from hypopneumia is not that the church members ask to be filled with the Holy Spirit too frequently, but that some of them don't ask at all. This is what needs to be corrected, starting at the level of pastoral leadership.

SPIRITUAL VITALITY HELPS THE IMMUNE SYSTEM

To go back to the illustration at the beginning of this chapter of comparing hypopneumia to vitamin deficiency, it is obvious that if the Holy Spirit is actively ministering in the church, susceptibility to other church diseases will be lessened. To a degree greater than any contextual factors or institutional factors, *spiritual* factors can permeate the whole church system to such an extent that many other things can be all but overlooked. This explains in part how some churches can seem to break many of the rules of church growth and still grow. The power of the Holy Spirit has given them an edge. Their spiritual immune system is above normal, and although the devil might try in many ways to prevent their growth, he is not successful. As John said, "He who is in you is greater than he who is in the world" (1 John 4:4).

I saved hypopneumia until last because its cure, namely receiving more of the active presence of the Holy Spirit in the church, is the most far-reaching cure of all. When the Holy Spirit comes to individuals and to the congregation as a whole, the fruit of the Spirit becomes evident in lives and the power of the Holy Spirit opens unlimited horizons for bringing new people to Christ, for the church to grow, and for the love of God to spread throughout the community.

Notes

1. J. Herbert Kane, *The Christian World Mission Today and Tomorrow* (Grand Rapids: Baker Book House, 1981), p. 212.
2. George Barna, *User Friendly Churches* (Ventura, Calif.: Regal Books, 1991), p. 116.
3. Thom S. Rainer, *Giant Awakenings* (Nashville: Broadman & Holman Publishers, 1995), p. 17.
4. Ibid.
5. Glen Martin and Gary McIntosh, *The Issachar Factor* (Nashville: Broadman & Holman Publishers, 1993), p. 31.
6. Ron Crandall, *Turnaround Strategies for the Small Church* (Nashville: Abingdon Press, 1995), p. 40.
7. Ibid., p. 43.
8. George Barna, *Turnaround Churches* (Ventura, Calif.: Regal Books, 1993), p. 97.

INDEX